Interactive Notebooks

SCIENCE

Grade 3

Credits

Author: Natalie Rompella
Content Editors: Elise Craver, Julie B. Killian, Christine Schwab, and Angela Triplett

Visit *carsondellosa.com* for correlations to Common Core, state, national, and Canadian provincial standards.

Carson-Dellosa Publishing LLC
PO Box 35665
Greensboro, NC 27425 USA
carsondellosa.com

978-1-4838-3123-7
02-261177784

Table of Contents

© Carson-Dellosa • CD-104907

What Are Interactive Notebooks?

Interactive notebooks are a unique form of note taking. Teachers guide students through creating pages of notes on new topics. Instead of being in the traditional linear, handwritten format, notes are colorful and spread across the pages. Notes also often include drawings, diagrams, and 3-D elements to make the material understandable and relevant. Students are encouraged to complete their notebook pages in ways that make sense to them. With this personalization, no two pages are exactly the same.

Because of their creative nature, interactive notebooks allow students to be active participants in their own learning. Teachers can easily differentiate pages to address the levels and needs of each learner. The notebooks are arranged sequentially, and students can create tables of contents as they create pages, making it simple for students to use their notebooks for reference throughout the year. The interactive, easily personalized format makes interactive notebooks ideal for engaging students in learning new concepts.

Using interactive notebooks can take as much or as little time as you like. Students will initially take longer to create pages but will get faster as they become familiar with the process of creating pages. You may choose to only create a notebook page as a class at the beginning of each unit, or you may choose to create a new page for each topic within a unit. You can decide what works best for your students and schedule.

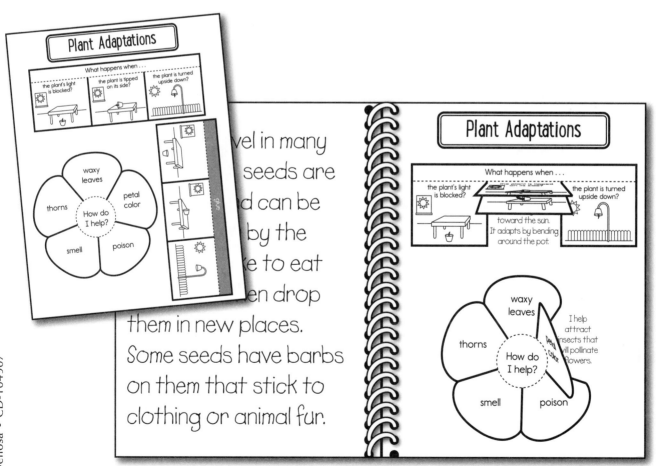

A student's interactive notebook for plant adaptations

Getting Started

You can start using interactive notebooks at any point in the school year. Use the following guidelines to help you get started in your classroom. (For more specific details, management ideas, and tips, see page 10.)

1. Plan each notebook.

Use the planning template (page 9) to lay out a general plan for the topics you plan to cover in each notebook for the year.

2. Choose a notebook type.

Interactive notebooks are usually either single-subject, spiral-bound notebooks, composition books, or three-ring binders with loose-leaf paper. Each type presents pros and cons. See page 5 for a more in-depth look at each type of notebook.

3. Allow students to personalize their notebooks.

Have students decorate their notebook covers, as well as add their names and subjects. This provides a sense of ownership and emphasizes the personalized nature of the notebooks.

4. Number the pages and create the table of contents.

Have students number the bottom outside corner of each page, front and back. When completing a new page, adding a table of contents entry will be easy. Have students title the first page of each notebook "Table of Contents." Have them leave several blank pages at the front of each notebook for the table of contents. Refer to your general plan for an idea of about how many entries students will be creating.

5. Start creating pages.

Always begin a new page by adding an entry to the table of contents. Create the first notebook pages along with students to model proper format and expectations.

This book contains individual topics for you to introduce. Use the pages in the order that best fits your curriculum. You may also choose to alter the content presented to better match your school's curriculum. The provided lesson plans often do not instruct students to add color. Students should make their own choices about personalizing the content in ways that make sense to them. Encourage students to highlight and color the pages as they desire while creating them.

After introducing topics, you may choose to add more practice pages. Use the reproducibles (pages 78–96) to easily create new notebook pages for practice or to introduce topics not addressed in this book.

Use the grading rubric (page 11) to grade students' interactive notebooks at various points throughout the year. Provide students copies of the rubric to glue into their notebooks and refer to as they create pages.

What Type of Notebook Should I Use?

Spiral Notebook

The pages in this book are formatted for a standard one-subject notebook.

Pros

- Notebook can be folded in half.
- Page size is larger.
- It is inexpensive.
- It often comes with pockets for storing materials.

Cons

- Pages can easily fall out.
- Spirals can snag or become misshapen.
- Page count and size vary widely.
- It is not as durable as a binder.

Tips

- Encase the spiral in duct tape to make it more durable.
- Keep the notebooks in a central place to prevent them from getting damaged in desks.

Composition Notebook

Pros

- Pages don't easily fall out.
- Page size and page count are standard.
- It is inexpensive.

Cons

- Notebook cannot be folded in half.
- Page size is smaller.
- It is not as durable as a binder.

Tips

- Copy pages meant for standard-sized notebooks at 85 or 90 percent. Test to see which works better for your notebook.

Binder with Loose-Leaf Paper

Pros

- Pages can be easily added, moved, or removed.
- Pages can be removed individually for grading.
- You can add full-page printed handouts.
- It has durable covers.

Cons

- Pages can easily fall out.
- Pages aren't durable.
- It is more expensive than a notebook.
- Students can easily misplace or lose pages.
- Larger size makes it more difficult to store.

Tips

- Provide hole reinforcers for damaged pages.

How to Organize an Interactive Notebook

You may organize an interactive notebook in many different ways. You may choose to organize it by unit and work sequentially through the book. Or, you may choose to create different sections that you will revisit and add to throughout the year. Choose the format that works best for your students and subject.

An interactive notebook includes different types of pages in addition to the pages students create. Non-content pages you may want to add include the following:

Title Page

This page is useful for quickly identifying notebooks. It is especially helpful in classrooms that use multiple interactive notebooks for different subjects. Have students write the subject (such as "Science") on the title page of each interactive notebook. They should also include their full names. You may choose to have them include other information such as the teacher's name, classroom number, or class period.

Table of Contents

The table of contents is an integral part of the interactive notebook. It makes referencing previously created pages quick and easy for students. Make sure that students leave several pages at the beginning of each notebook for a table of contents.

Expectations and Grading Rubric

It is helpful for each student to have a copy of the expectations for creating interactive notebook pages. You may choose to include a list of expectations for parents and students to sign, as well as a grading rubric (page 11).

Unit Title Pages

Consider using a single page at the beginning of each section to separate it. Title the page with the unit name. Add a tab (page 78) to the edge of the page to make it easy to flip to the unit. Add a table of contents for only the pages in that unit.

Glossary

Reserve a six-page section at the back of the notebook where students can create a glossary. Draw a line to split in half the front and back of each page, creating 24 sections. Combine Q and R and Y and Z to fit the entire alphabet. Have students add an entry as each new vocabulary word is introduced.

Formatting Student Notebook Pages

The other major consideration for planning an interactive notebook is how to treat the left and right sides of a notebook spread. Interactive journals are usually viewed with the notebook open flat. This creates a left side and a right side. You have several options for how to treat the two sides of the spread.

Traditionally, the right side is used for the teacher-directed part of the lesson, and the left side is used for students to interact with the lesson content. The lessons in this book use this format. However, you may prefer to switch the order for your class so that the teacher-directed learning is on the left and the student input is on the right.

It can also be important to include standards, learning objectives, or essential questions in interactive notebooks. You may choose to write these on the top-left side of each page before completing the teacher-directed page on the right side. You may also choose to have students include the "Introduction" part of each lesson in that same top-left section. This is the *in, through, out* method. Students enter *in* the lesson on the top left of the page, go *through* the lesson on the right page, and exit *out* of the lesson on the bottom left with a reflection activity.

The following chart details different types of items and activities that you could include on each side.

Left Side Student Output	**Right Side** Teacher-Directed Learning
• learning objectives	• vocabulary and definitions
• essential questions	• mini-lessons
• I Can statements	• folding activities
• brainstorming	• steps in a process
• making connections	• example problems
• summarizing	• notes
• making conclusions	• diagrams
• practice problems	• graphic organizers
• opinions	• hints and tips
• questions	• big ideas
• mnemonics	
• drawings and diagrams	

Planning for the Year

Making a general plan for interactive notebooks will help with planning, grading, and testing throughout the year. You do not need to plan every single page, but knowing what topics you will cover and in what order can be helpful in many ways.

Use the Interactive Notebook Plan (page 9) to plan your units and topics and where they should be placed in the notebooks. Remember to include enough pages at the beginning for the non-content pages, such as the title page, table of contents, and grading rubric. You may also want to leave a page at the beginning of each unit to place a mini table of contents for just that section.

In addition, when planning new pages, it can be helpful to sketch the pieces you will need to create. Use the following notebook template and notes to plan new pages.

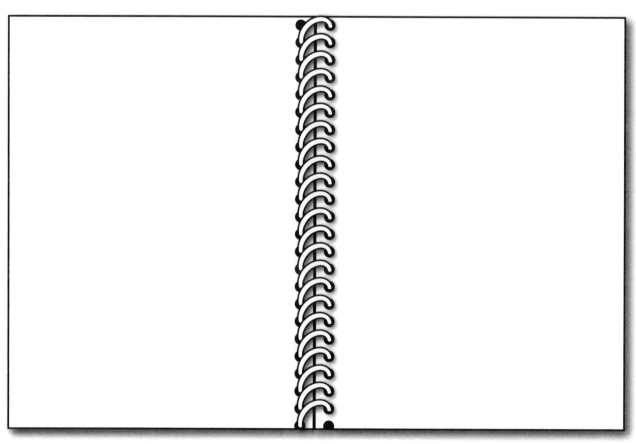

Left Side   **Right Side**

Notes

_____

_____

_____

Interactive Notebook Plan

Page	Topic	Page	Topic
1		51	
2		52	
3		53	
4		54	
5		55	
6		56	
7		57	
8		58	
9		59	
10		60	
11		61	
12		62	
13		63	
14		64	
15		65	
16		66	
17		67	
18		68	
19		69	
20		70	
21		71	
22		72	
23		73	
24		74	
25		75	
26		76	
27		77	
28		78	
29		79	
30		80	
31		81	
32		82	
33		83	
34		84	
35		85	
36		86	
37		87	
38		88	
39		89	
40		90	
41		91	
42		92	
43		93	
44		94	
45		95	
46		96	
47		97	
48		98	
49		99	
50		100	

Managing Interactive Notebooks in the Classroom

Working with Younger Students

- Use your yearly plan to preprogram a table of contents that you can copy and give to students to glue into their notebooks, instead of writing individual entries.

- Have assistants or parent volunteers precut pieces.

- Create glue sponges to make gluing easier. Place large sponges in plastic containers with white glue. The sponges will absorb the glue. Students can wipe the backs of pieces across the sponges to apply the glue with less mess.

Creating Notebook Pages

- For storing loose pieces, add a pocket to the inside back cover. Use the envelope pattern (page 81), an envelope, a jumbo library pocket, or a resealable plastic bag. Or, tape the bottom and side edges of the two last pages of the notebook together to create a large pocket.

- When writing under flaps, have students trace the outline of each flap so that they can visualize the writing boundary.

- Where the dashed line will be hidden on the inside of the fold, have students first fold the piece in the opposite direction so that they can see the dashed line. Then, students should fold the piece back the other way along the same fold line to create the fold in the correct direction.

- To avoid losing pieces, have students keep all of their scraps on their desks until they have finished each page.

- To contain paper scraps and avoid multiple trips to the trash can, provide small groups with small buckets or tubs.

- For students who run out of room, keep full and half sheets available. Students can glue these to the bottom of the pages and fold them up when not in use.

Dealing with Absences

- Create a model notebook for absent students to reference when they return to school.

- Have students cut a second set of pieces as they work on their own pages.

Using the Notebook

- To organize sections of the notebook, provide each student with a sheet of tabs (page 78).

- To easily find the next blank page, either cut off the top-right corner of each page as it is used or attach a long piece of yarn or ribbon to the back cover to be used as a bookmark.

Interactive Notebook Grading Rubric

4

_____ Table of contents is complete.

_____ All notebook pages are included.

_____ All notebook pages are complete.

_____ Notebook pages are neat and organized.

_____ Information is correct.

_____ Pages show personalization, evidence of learning, and original ideas.

3

_____ Table of contents is mostly complete.

_____ One notebook page is missing.

_____ Notebook pages are mostly complete.

_____ Notebook pages are mostly neat and organized.

_____ Information is mostly correct.

_____ Pages show some personalization, evidence of learning, and original ideas.

2

_____ Table of contents is missing a few entries.

_____ A few notebook pages are missing.

_____ A few notebook pages are incomplete.

_____ Notebook pages are somewhat messy and unorganized.

_____ Information has several errors.

_____ Pages show little personalization, evidence of learning, or original ideas.

1

_____ Table of contents is incomplete.

_____ Many notebook pages are missing.

_____ Many notebook pages are incomplete.

_____ Notebook pages are too messy and unorganized to use.

_____ Information is incorrect.

_____ Pages show no personalization, evidence of learning, or original ideas.

Plant Parts

Introduction

Have students name the parts of a plant (flower, leaves, stem, roots, stamen, pistil, petals, and sepals). Write them on the board. Have a student describe a plant part without naming it and have the rest of the class guess which plant part the student is describing.

Creating the Notebook Page

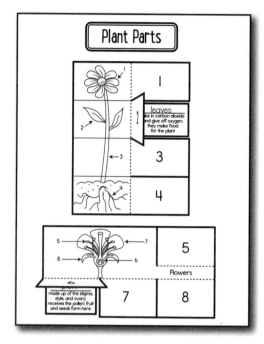

Guide students through the following steps to complete the right-hand page in their notebooks.

1. Add a Table of Contents entry for the Plant Parts pages.

2. Cut out the title and glue it to the top of the page.

3. Cut out the tall flower flap book. Cut on the solid lines to create four flaps. Apply glue to the back of the left section and attach it below the title.

4. Cut out the *Flowers* flap book. Cut on the solid lines to create four flaps. Apply glue to the back of the flower section and right center section. Attach the flap book to the bottom of the page.

5. Cut out the definition pieces. Read each definition and decide which plant part it describes. Fill in the blank with the name of the correct plant part.

6. Glue each definition under the flap that corresponds to the correct plant part.

Reflect on Learning

To complete the left-hand page, have students use words from the right-hand page to write a paragraph summarizing how the parts of a plant help it grow.

Answer Key
1. flower: where pollination takes place; creates seeds; 2. leaves: take in carbon dioxide and give off oxygen; they make food for the plant; 3. stem: gives a plant support; allows water and nutrients to get to other plant parts; 4. roots: absorb water and nutrients from the soil and draw them up to the rest of the plant; 5. stamen: made up of the anther and filament; produces pollen; 6. pistil: made up of the stigma, style, and ovary; receives the pollen; fruit and seeds form here; 7. petals: help attract pollinators; 8. sepals: protect the flower before it opens

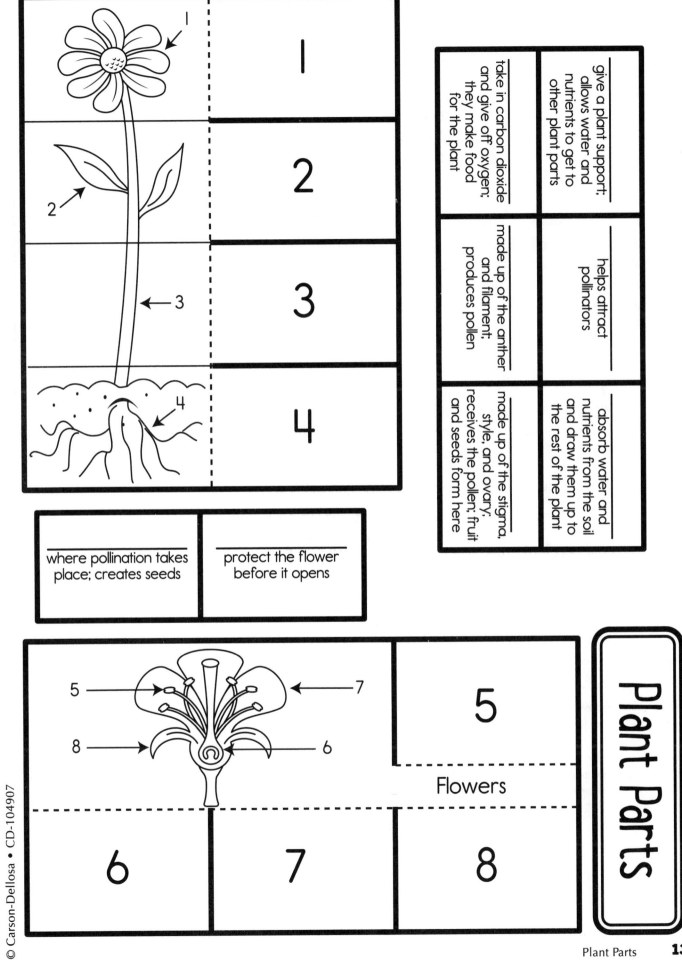

1	
	2
	3
	4

give a plant support;
allows water and
nutrients to get to
other plant parts

take in carbon dioxide
and give off oxygen;
they make food
for the plant

helps attract
pollinators

made up of the anther
and filament;
produces pollen

absorb water and
nutrients from the soil
and draw them up to
the rest of the plant

made up of the stigma,
style, and ovary;
receives the pollen; fruit
and seeds form here

where pollination takes
place; creates seeds

protect the flower
before it opens

5	Flowers
6	7	8

Plant Parts

Plant Adaptations

Introduction

Distribute self-stick notes. Have each student write a plant adaptation on a self-stick note. Then, give a scenario such as "There is a drought" or "a plant wants to be pollinated." Have students who have adaptations that help with this hold up their notes.

Creating the Notebook Page

Guide students through the following steps to complete the right-hand page in their notebooks.

1. Add a Table of Contents entry for the Plant Adaptations pages.

2. Cut out the title and glue it to the top of the page.

3. Cut out the *What happens when . . .* flap book and the three scenes flap book. Cut on the solid lines to create three flaps on each. Apply glue to the gray glue section and place the *What happens when . . .* flap book on top to create a stacked six flap book. Apply glue to the back of the top section and attach the stacked flap book below the title.

4. Read the scenario on each flap. Under the flap, complete the scene by drawing the plant and how it would grow in order to adapt to the situation. Under the scenes flaps, write what happened and tell why.

5. Cut out the flower flap book. Cut on the solid lines to create five flaps. Apply glue to the back of the center section and attach it to the bottom of the page.

6. Under each flap, tell how the adaptation helps the plant.

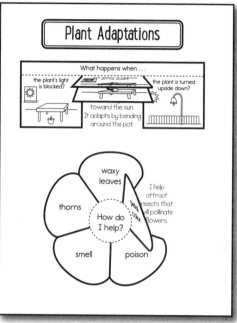

Reflect on Learning

To complete the left-hand page, have students tell what adaptations different seeds have.

Answer Key
First frame: plant should bend around table toward sun; Second frame: plant should grow upward toward sun; Third frame: flowered end of plant should grow upward toward sun, while the roots should grow downward

Plant Adaptations

What happens when . . .

the plant's light is blocked?

the plant is tipped on its side?

the plant is turned upside down?

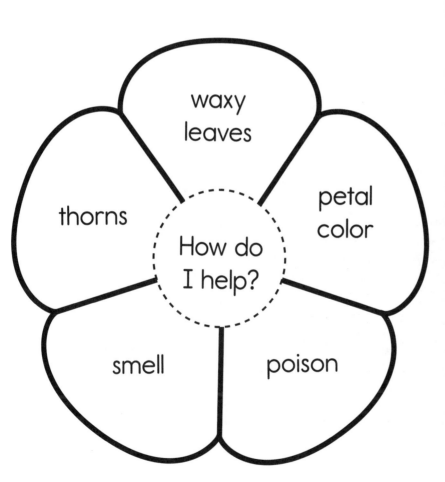

waxy leaves

petal color

thorns

How do I help?

smell

poison

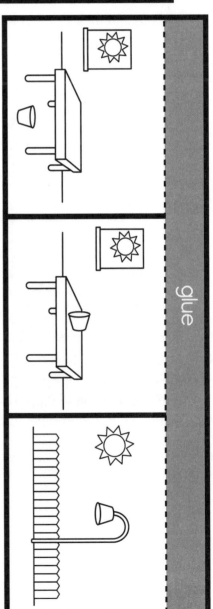

glue

Animal Classification

Introduction

Distribute self-stick notes so that each student gets two. Have students write the name of a kind of animal on each self-stick note. Have students work in small groups to sort their animals. Allow groups to discuss their sorting methods. Tell students that animals can be divided into groups based on characteristics. Discuss what characteristics are used to classify animals.

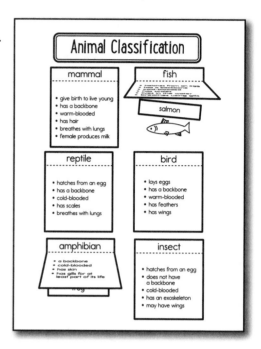

Creating the Notebook Page

Guide students through the following steps to complete the right-hand page in their notebooks.

1. Add a Table of Contents entry for the Animal Classification pages.

2. Cut out the title and glue it to the top of the page.

3. Cut out the six flaps. Apply glue to the back of the top sections and attach them to the page.

4. Cut out the six animal names.

5. Using the descriptions, decide which group each animal belongs to. Glue it under the correct flap, leaving room for drawing or writing.

6. Under each flap, write or draw a picture of the animal group that is being described: fish, mammal, reptile, amphibian, bird, or insect. (Note: There are exceptions to some characteristics for certain species. For example, although snakes are reptiles, some give birth to live young.)

Reflect on Learning

To complete the left-hand page, draw a three-circle Venn diagram on the board. Have students copy the diagram and use it to compare and contrast three animal groups.

Answer Key
amphibian: frog; bird: chicken; insect: dragonfly; mammal: human; fish: salmon; reptile: turtle

Animal Classification

amphibian

- a backbone
- cold-blooded
- has skin
- has gills for at least part of its life

bird

- lays eggs
- has a backbone
- warm-blooded
- has feathers
- has wings

insect

- hatches from an egg
- does not have a backbone
- cold-blooded
- has an exoskeleton
- may have wings

mammal

- give birth to live young
- has a backbone
- warm-blooded
- has hair
- breathes with lungs
- female produces milk

fish

- hatches from an egg
- has a backbone
- cold-blooded
- has scales
- lives in the water
- breathes using gills

reptile

- hatches from an egg
- has a backbone
- cold-blooded
- has scales
- breathes with lungs

chicken	dragonfly
human	salmon
frog	turtle

Animal Adaptations

Introduction

Have students get into groups of about four and choose an animal. Have them think about and discuss the adaptations that animal has for finding food, escaping predators, and keeping warm. Students can then share with the rest of the class what they discussed about their animals' adaptions.

Creating the Notebook Page

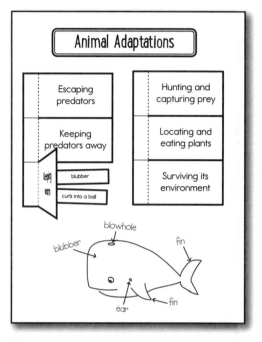

Guide students through the following steps to complete the right-hand page in their notebooks.

1. Add a Table of Contents entry for the Animal Adaptations pages.

2. Cut out the title and glue it to the top of the page.

3. Cut out the two flap books. Cut on the solid lines to create three flaps on each. Apply glue to the back of the left section of the flap books and attach them side by side below the title.

4. Cut out the 18 adaptation pieces.

5. Read the six flaps. Decide how each adaptation might help an animal fulfill its needs. Glue each adaptation under the correct flap. Some adaptations may help in more than one way. You may write the adaptations under any other flaps they help with.

6. Write any other adaptations you think of so that each flap has at least five adaptations.

7. Draw a picture of an animal at the bottom of the page below the flap books. Label each of its adaptations.

Reflect on Learning

To complete the left-hand page, have students create a T-chart listing human adaptations and what they are useful for.

Answer Key
Answers will vary but may include: Escaping predators: quick, fins; Keeping predators away: spines/spikes; Keeping warm: curls into a ball, blubber; Hunting and capturing prey: quick, poison, sharp teeth; Locating and eating plants: good sense of smell, teeth for grinding food, can see ultraviolet light; Surviving its environment: sees in the dark, echolocation, fins, digs underground, thick skin, no spine, blubber

Animal Adaptations

quick	digs underground	poison
large ears	sharp teeth	hooves
curls into a ball	good sense of smell	spines/spikes
teeth for grinding food	stinger	can see ultraviolet light
sees in the dark	thick skin	echolocation
no spine	fins	blubber

Escaping predators

Keeping predators away

Keeping warm

Hunting and capturing prey

Locating and eating plants

Surviving its environment

Life Cycles

Each student will need a brass paper fastener to complete this page.

Introduction

Have a student tell about the life cycle of a dog (baby, pup, adult). Ask if all animal life cycles are the same. Have students give examples of any that are different from the dog's life cycle. Ask how a plant's life cycle is different from animals' life cycles.

Creating the Notebook Page

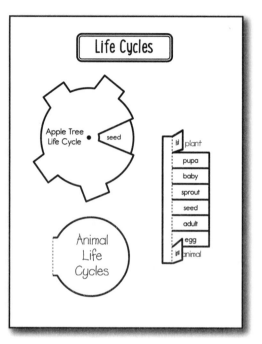

Guide students through the following steps to complete the right-hand page in their notebooks.

1. Add a Table of Contents entry for the Life Cycles pages.

2. Cut out the title and glue it to the top of the page.

3. Cut out the circle with six words. These are the stages of an apple tree's life cycle.

4. Cut out the *Apple Tree Life Cycle* piece. Push a brass paper fastener into the center of the *Apple Tree Life Cycle* piece and into the center of the circle with six words. It may be helpful to create the holes in each piece first. Apply glue to the back of the top piece's tabs and attach it below and to the left of the title. The brass paper fastener should not go through the page, and the piece underneath should spin freely.

5. Discuss the stages. If desired, draw a picture for each apple tree life cycle stage on the page.

6. Cut out the double circle book. Fold on the dashed lines to close the book. Apply glue to the back of the *Chicken Life Cycle* section and attach it to the bottom left of the page.

7. Write *Animal Life Cycles* on the front of the book. Label the stages of the *Chicken Life Cycle*.

8. Cut out the flap book. Cut on the solid lines to create eight flaps. Apply glue to the back of the left section and attach it to the right side of the page.

9. Under each flap, write whether the word relates to a plant or an animal's life cycle.

Reflect on Learning

To complete the left-hand page, have students answer the following questions: What is similar about the beetle and the chicken life cycles? What is similar about the chicken and the apple tree life cycles?

Answer Key
Chicken Life Cycle: egg, chick, adult (chicken); fruit: plant; pupa: animal; baby: animal; sprout: plant; seed: plant; adult: animal; egg: animal; larva: animal

Life Cycles

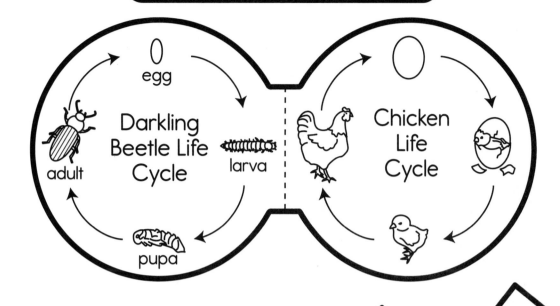

Darkling Beetle Life Cycle
egg
larva
pupa
adult

Chicken Life Cycle

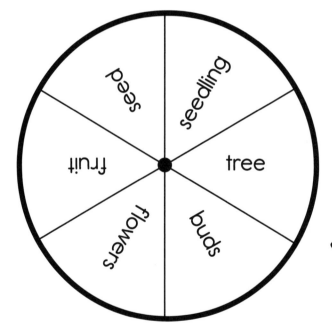

seed
seedling
tree
buds
flowers
fruit

Apple Tree Life Cycle

fruit | pupa | baby | sprout | seed | adult | egg | larva

Food Chains

Introduction

Ask students what a food chain is. Discuss that although plants are often thought of as the beginning of the food chain, the sun actually provides energy for plants. Have five or so students come to the front of the class. Have the first student be the sun. Have the next student name a producer. Have the third student name a consumer of that. Have several more students try to continue the food chain.

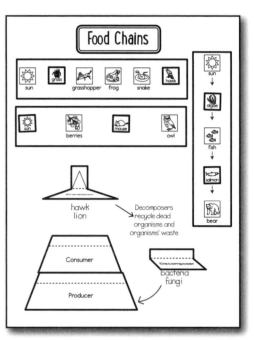

Creating the Notebook Page

Guide students through the following steps to complete the right-hand page in their notebooks.

1. Add a Table of Contents entry for the Food Chains pages.

2. Cut out the title and glue it to the top of the page.

3. Cut out the three food chain strips. Glue the strips with the grasshopper and the the berries below and to the left of the title. Glue the strip with the bear along the right side of the page.

4. Cut out the six pictures. Look at the blank squares on the three food chains. Glue the correct picture in each blank to complete the food chains.

5. Cut out the *Predator, Consumer,* and *Producer* flaps. Fit them together so that they form a triangle. Apply glue to the back of the top section of each piece and attach the flaps to the bottom-left side of the page.

6. Cut out the *Decomposer* flap. Apply glue to the back of the top section and attach it next to the triangle.

7. Under each flap, give examples of that type of organism. Add arrows to show the relationship between decomposers and the organisms in the triangle. Discuss the flow of energy in a food chain. If desired, discuss how decomposers can enter a food chain at any point. For example, decomposers can decompose producers or consumers.

Reflect on Learning

To complete the left-hand page, draw a food chain that includes people as predators.

Answer Key
sun > berries > mouse > owl; sun > grass > grasshopper > frog > snake > hawk; sun > algae > fish > salmon > bear

Food Chains

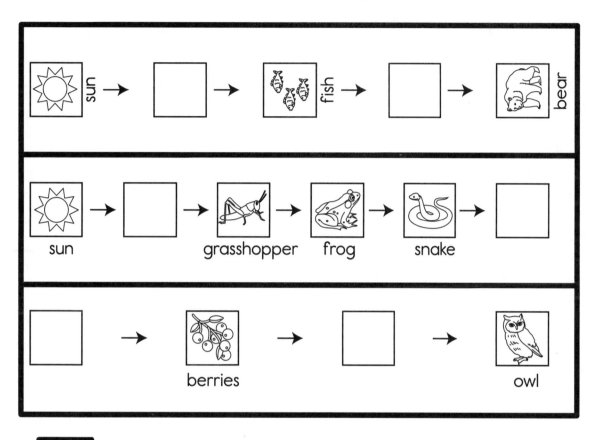

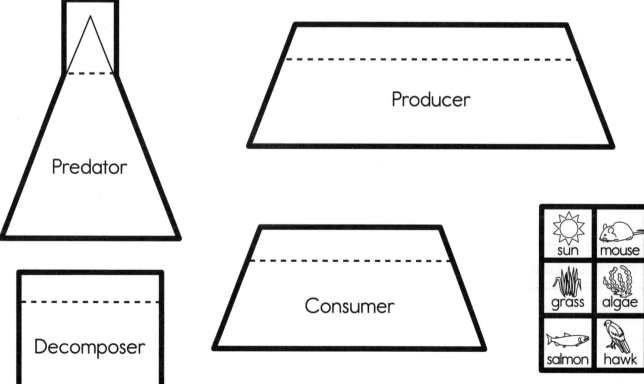

Interdependence

Students will need a sharpened pencil and a paper clip to complete the spinner activity.

Introduction

Ask students for an example of an interaction between a plant and an animal. Discuss what this relationship helps: the plant, the animal, or both. Ask whether there are any relationships where one of the organisms doesn't get anything. Distribute index cards. Have each student write an example of a relationship between two organisms on a card. As a class, categorize the relationships as to whether both organisms are helped, one is helped while the other is harmed, or one is helped while the other is not affected.

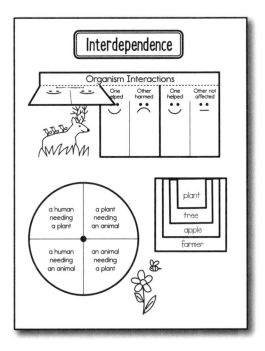

Creating the Notebook Page

Guide students through the following steps to complete the right-hand page in their notebooks.

1. Add a Table of Contents entry for the Interdependence pages.

2. Cut out the title and glue it to the top of the page.

3. Cut out the *Organism Interactions* flap book. Cut on the solid lines to create three flaps. Apply glue to the back of the top section and attach it below the title.

4. Under each flap, draw or write an example of that type of relationship.

5. Cut out the circle. Glue it to the bottom of the page.

6. Use a sharpened pencil and a paper clip to create a spinner. Spin the paper clip. When the paper clip lands on a phrase, think of an example of that type of relationship. Draw a small picture of it beside the circle. Add another small picture each time you spin.

7. Cut out the four squares. Apply glue to the gray glue section of each box and place one on top of the other to create a stacked piece. Glue it to the page beside the spinner. Write an organism name such as *plant* on the top square. Then, on each of the following squares, write the chain of interaction of the organism such as *tree, apple, farmer.*

Reflect on Learning

To complete the left-hand page, have students choose an ecosystem or biome such as a forest, desert, or tundra. Have students list four or more interdependent relationships that would occur there.

Interdependence

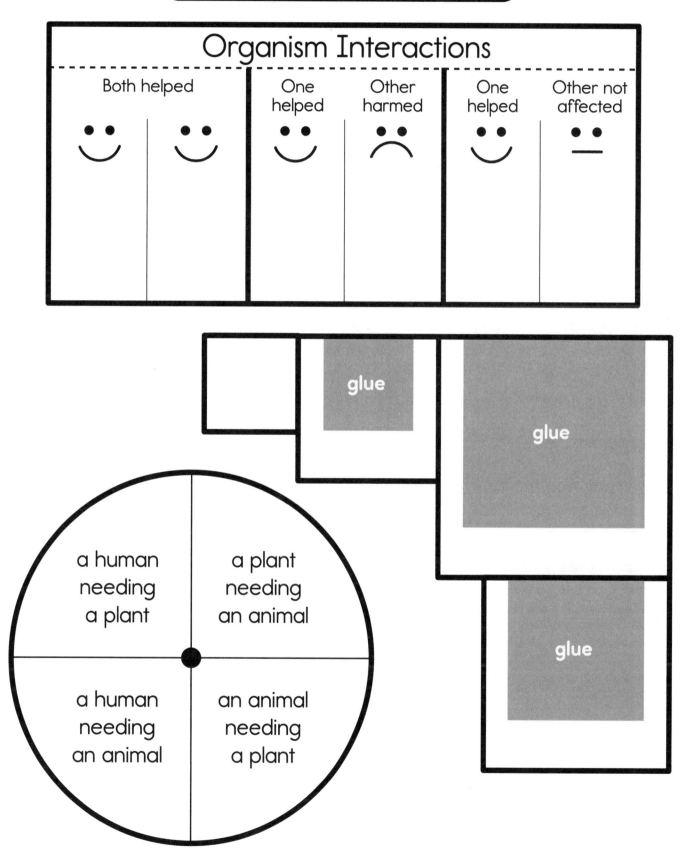

Organism Interactions

Both helped	One helped	Other harmed	One helped	Other not affected

glue

glue

glue

a human needing a plant

a plant needing an animal

a human needing an animal

an animal needing a plant

Response to Seasons

Introduction

Review the four seasons and what the weather is like in each. Ask students whether plants and animals do different things in the different seasons. Have students brainstorm a list of plant and animal responses to the seasonal changes. Have one student from each group share her list.

Creating the Notebook Page

Guide students through the following steps to complete the right-hand page in their notebooks.

1. Add a Table of Contents entry for the Response to Seasons pages.

2. Cut out the title and glue it to the top of the page.

3. Cut out the Seasons flap book. Cut on the solid lines to create four flaps. Apply glue to the back of the center section and attach it to the middle of the page.

4. Cut out the 17 action strips.

5. Read each action. Decide in which season it occurs and glue it under that flap. (Note: An action may apply to more than one season.)

6. On the bottom of the page, write four sentences about the seasons. Each sentence should describe one response an organism may have to that season.

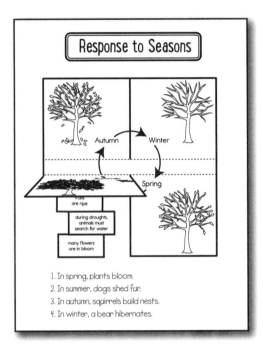

Response to Seasons

Autumn   Winter

Spring

fruits are ripe

during droughts, animals must search for water

many flowers are in bloom

1. In spring, plants bloom.
2. In summer, dogs shed fur.
3. In autumn, squirrels build nests.
4. In winter, a bear hibernates.

Reflect on Learning

To complete the left-hand page, have students choose one season to draw a picture about. Have students show what occurs during that season in nature and label what is happening.

Answer Key
Autumn: trees lose leaves, animals put on weight, animals store food, animals migrate to warmer climates, sap moves to the roots of trees; Winter: animals develop thicker or different-colored coats of fur, animals hibernate or sleep for long periods of time, plants do not grow; Spring: baby animals are born, animals shed thick fur coats, animals make nests and dens, animals migrate back, some flowers begin to bloom, tree leaves grow; Summer: many flowers are in bloom, fruits are ripe, animals must search for water during droughts

Autumn → Winter

Summer → Spring

Winter → Spring

Autumn ← Summer

trees lose leaves	animals migrate to warmer climates
baby animals are born	fruits are ripe
many flowers are in bloom	some flowers begin to bloom
animals develop thicker or different-colored coats of fur	sap moves to the roots of trees
animals hibernate or sleep for long periods of time	tree leaves grow
animals store food	animals put on weight
animals shed thick fur coats	during droughts, animals must search for water
animals make nests and dens	plants do not grow
animals migrate back	

The Human Body

Introduction

On large craft paper or on the board, trace the outline of a student. Ask the class what systems make up the human body (such as digestive, skeletal, muscular, circulatory, respiratory, and nervous). Write the system names on the board. Use different colors of markers to draw each system on the model. Have students come up and label the parts to that system.

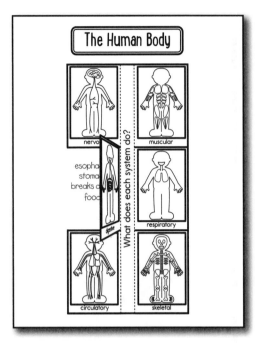

Creating the Notebook Page

Guide students through the following steps to complete the right-hand page in their notebooks.

1. Add a Table of Contents entry for The Human Body pages.

2. Cut out the title and glue it to the top of the page.

3. Cut out the flap book. Cut on the solid lines to create six flaps. Apply glue to the back of the center section and attach it to the page.

4. Cut out the six body systems illustrations. Glue each illustration to the front of the correct flap.

5. Under each flap, write words that have to do with the system. Use words such as body part names and action words (pumps blood, breaks down food, etc.). You may also describe what function(s) the system performs for the body.

Reflect on Learning

To complete the left-hand page, draw a Venn diagram on the board and have students copy it. Have them compare two body systems.

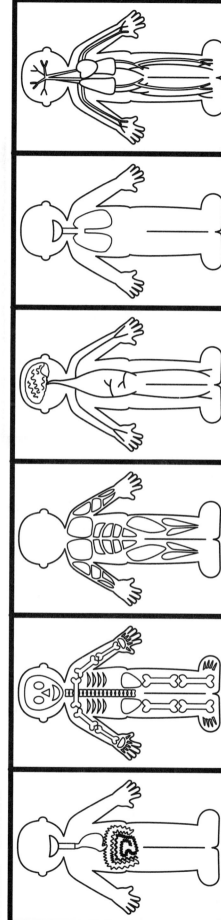

	What does each system do?	
nervous		muscular
digestive		respiratory
circulatory		skeletal

Growth and Repair

Introduction

Discuss with students the changes that occur when a puppy grows into an adult dog (gets taller, teeth fall out, and nails grow). Discuss how organisms grow and change. Ask what evidence there is that our own bodies are able to heal and grow.

Creating the Notebook Page

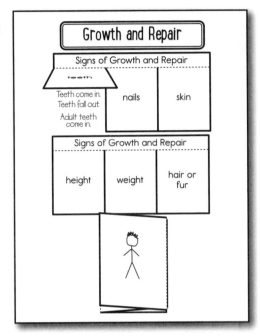

Guide students through the following steps to complete the right-hand page in their notebooks.

1. Add a Table of Contents entry for the Growth and Repair pages.

2. Cut out the title and glue it to the top of the page.

3. Cut out the two *Signs of Growth and Repair* flap books. Cut on the solid lines to create three flaps on each. Apply glue to the back of the top sections and attach them below the title.

4. Under each flap, tell different changes that can occur with each feature. (For example, for teeth: milk teeth come in and fall out, and adult teeth come in.)

5. Cut out the three-part accordion fold. Fold on the dashed lines, alternating the fold direction. Apply glue to the back of the third section and attach it to the bottom of the page.

6. In the first section, draw a picture of a person or animal. In the second section, show two changes to that person or animal; they can be from growth, injury, or recovery. In the third section, show two additional changes. Label what is happening in each.

Reflect on Learning

To complete the left-hand page, have students use the three pictures they drew to tell a story about what happened to the person or animal over time.

Signs of Growth and Repair

teeth	nails	skin

Signs of Growth and Repair

height	weight	hair or fur

Growth and Repair

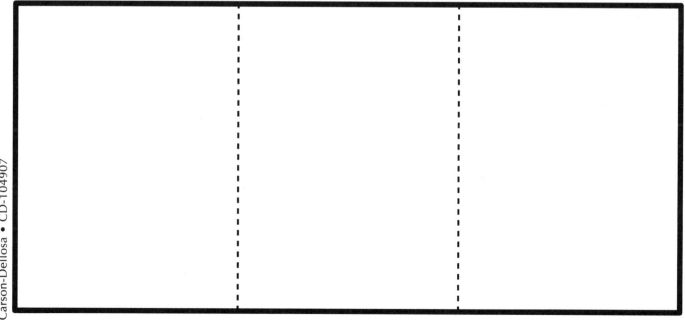

Traits

Introduction

Discuss with students the kind of traits people get from their parents. Talk about traits that are learned. Create a list of people they might have learned these traits from. As a class, consider one inherited trait such as being able to roll one's tongue. Take a class tally of how many students can and how many cannot.

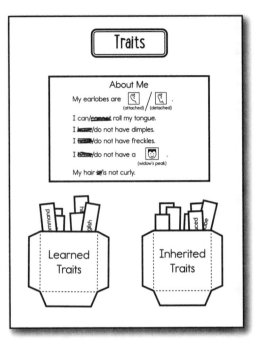

Creating the Notebook Page

Guide students through the following steps to complete the right-hand page in their notebooks.

1. Add a Table of Contents entry for the Traits pages.

2. Cut out the title and glue it to the top of the page.

3. Cut out the *About Me* piece. Glue it to the page below the title.

4. Read each sentence. Cross out the incorrect parts of the sentence.

5. Cut out the *Learned Traits* and *Inherited Traits* pockets. Apply glue to the back of the tabs and attach the pockets to the bottom of the page.

6. Cut out the 14 traits.

7. Decide if each trait is learned or inherited and place it in the correct pocket.

Reflect on Learning

To complete the left-hand page, have students create a list of four inherited traits of a particular animal.

Answer Key
Learned Traits: hairstyle, dog sitting on command, knowing how to play soccer, speaking English, length of hair; Inherited Traits: eye color, type of seed produced, beak length, curly hair, hibernating in winter, type of earlobe, fur color, hair color, leaf shape

© Carson-Dellosa • CD-104907

About Me

My earlobes are 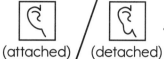 .

(attached) / (detached)

I can/cannot roll my tongue.

I have/do not have dimples.

I have/do not have freckles.

I have/do not have a .

(widow's peak)

My hair is/is not curly.

Traits

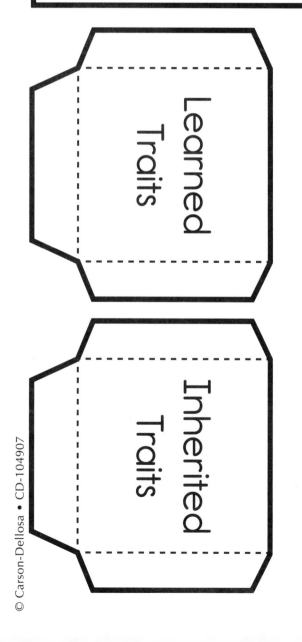

Learned Traits

Inherited Traits

eye color	type of earlobe
hairstyle	fur color
type of seed produced	knowing how to play soccer
beak length	speaking English
dog sitting on command	length of hair
curly hair	hair color
hibernating in winter	leaf shape

States of Matter

Introduction

Ask students to define matter. Ask what the three common states of matter are. Discuss the difference between a liquid such as water and a solid such as ice. Ask what water is in its gaseous state (water vapor). In small groups, have students create three-column T-charts to list as many solids, liquids, and gases as they can in five minutes. Have groups share some of their more unusual choices with the class.

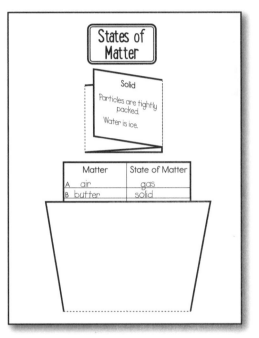

Creating the Notebook Page

Guide students through the following steps to complete the right-hand page in their notebooks.

1. Add a Table of Contents entry for the States of Matter pages.

2. Cut out the title and glue it to the top of the page.

3. Cut out the *Solid, Liquid, Gas* accordion fold. Fold on the dashed lines, alternating the fold direction so that the *Solid* section is on top. Apply glue to the back of the *Gas* section and attach it below the title.

4. On the three pages of the accordion book, write facts about solids, liquids, and gases, such as particle size and what water is like in each state.

5. Cut out the *Matter* alphabet book. Apply glue to the back of the top section and attach it to the bottom of the page.

6. For each letter of the alphabet, write something that begins with that letter. Next to the word, write whether it is a solid, a liquid, or a gas. Try to have a variety of states of matter. Fold it closed on the dashed line.

Reflect on Learning

To complete the left-hand page, have students explain how they know whether something is a solid, a liquid, or a gas.

States of Matter

Solid

Liquid

Gas

	Matter	State of Matter
A		
B		
C		
D		
E		
F		
G		
H		
I		
J		
K		
L		
M		
N		
O		
P		
Q		
R		
S		
T		
U		
V		
W		
X		
Y		
Z		

Properties of Matter

Introduction

Discuss various properties of matter such as texture, size, and weight. Bring in an assortment of objects. Have students describe the objects. Hide the objects in a container. Choose a student to secretly pull an object from the container and, without naming its color or shape, describe it to the rest of the class for them to guess.

Creating the Notebook Page

Guide students through the following steps to complete the right-hand page in their notebooks.

1. Add a Table of Contents entry for the Properties of Matter pages.

2. Cut out the title and glue it to the top of the page.

3. Cut out the *What are my properties?* flap book. Cut on the solid lines to create six flaps. Apply glue to the back of the middle section and attach it below the title.

4. Under each flap, write a list of properties for each object, such as *floats in water, is heavy, has spikes*, etc.

5. Cut out the *Different Properties of Matter* hexagon. Cut on the solid lines to create six flaps. Apply glue to the back of the middle section and attach it to the bottom of the page.

6. Under each flap, list the different forms of that property. For textures, list various textures, such as rough, bumpy, etc. Repeat for each property.

Reflect on Learning

To complete the left-hand page, write the following properties on the board: *heavy, black, smooth*. Have students draw two objects that fit this description.

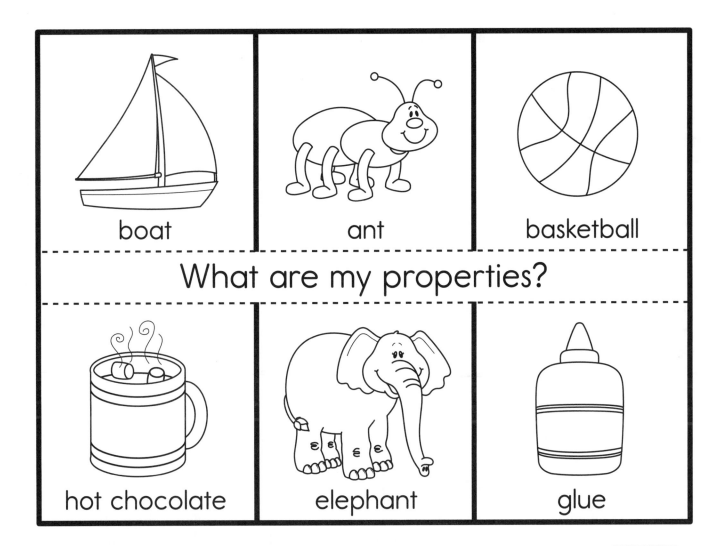

boat

ant

basketball

What are my properties?

hot chocolate

elephant

glue

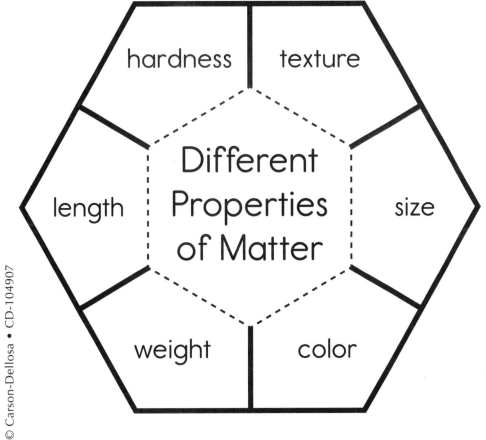

hardness

texture

length

Different Properties of Matter

size

weight

color

Changing Matter

Each student will need a brass paper fastener to complete this page.

Introduction

On index cards, write examples of matter changing forms, such as *butter melting, water freezing, dew on grass evaporating,* and *water condensing on the outside of a glass.* As a class, discuss ways matter changes (melts, condenses, evaporates, and freezes). Have volunteers come to the board, each choose an index card, and draw the action on the card without speaking. Have the rest of the class guess how matter is changing.

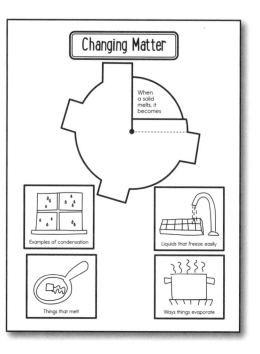

Creating the Notebook Page

Guide students through the following steps to complete the right-hand page in their notebooks.

1. Add a Table of Contents entry for the Changing Matter pages.

2. Cut out the title and glue it to the top of the page.

3. Cut out the circle and the tabbed piece. Be sure to cut on the solid line of the tabbed piece to form a flap. Push a brass paper fastener into the center of the tabbed piece and then through the center of the circle to attach them. It may be helpful to create the hole in each piece separately first. Apply glue to the back of the top piece's tabs and attach it below the title. The brass paper fastener should not go through the page, and the circle beneath should spin freely.

4. Move the circle so that it displays one of the ways matter can change. Read the sentence and silently answer how it changes. Check your answer by lifting the flap.

5. Cut out the four rectangular pieces. Glue them to the page.

6. Draw a picture on each piece to show examples of the four ways matter changes.

Reflect on Learning

To complete the left-hand page, have students explain how they could get the following to happen: water to change to ice, water to change to water vapor, ice to change to water, and water vapor to change to water.

Changing Matter

When a gas condenses, it becomes a liquid.

When a liquid evaporates, it becomes a gas.

When a solid melts, it becomes a liquid.

When a liquid freezes, it becomes a solid.

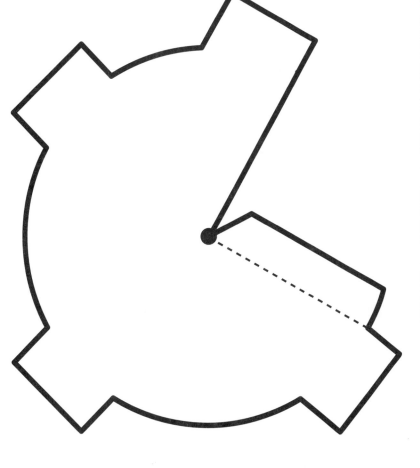

Examples of condensation

Things that melt

Ways things evaporate

Liquids that freeze easily

Force

Introduction

Set a ruler on a desk or table so that all the students can see it. Ask for thoughts about the ways the ruler can be moved without picking it up, such as pulling it with a string, pushing it with your hand, etc. For each way, discuss whether it is an example of a push or a pull.

Creating the Notebook Page

Guide students through the following steps to complete the right-hand page in their notebooks.

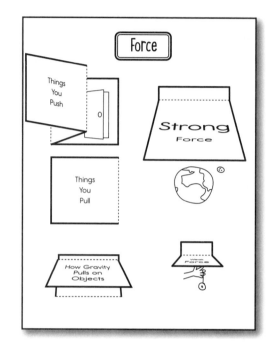

1. Add a Table of Contents entry for the Force pages.

2. Cut out the title and glue it to the top of the page.

3. Cut out the *Things You Push* and the *Things You Pull* accordion folds. Fold on the dashed lines, alternating the fold direction so that the titles are on top. Apply glue to the back of the last sections and attach them below and to the left of the title, one below the other.

4. Open the folds. On the blank pages, draw two examples of things you push and two examples of things you pull.

5. Cut out the *Strong Force* and *Weak Force* flaps. Apply glue to the back of the top sections and attach them below and to the right of the title.

6. Draw an example under each flap.

7. Cut out the *How Gravity Pulls* accordion fold. Fold on the dashed lines, alternating the fold direction so that the title is on the front. Apply glue to the back of the last section and attach it to the bottom left of the page.

8. Starting in the top section and ending in the section above the title, draw a comic strip showing gravity pulling on an object as if it were happening in slow motion.

Reflect on Learning

To complete the left-hand page, have students draw a playground and label whether each piece of playground equipment uses the force of a push, a pull, or both.

Force

Strong
Force

Weak
Force

Things
You
Pull

Things
You
Push

How Gravity
Pulls on
Objects

Motion

Each student will need a sharpened pencil and a paper clip to complete the spinner activity.

Introduction

Fill a small cup or glass to the top with water. Ask students what would happen if you walked briskly while holding the glass and then stopped abruptly. If possible, demonstrate. Help students understand why the water spilled (although you stopped your own motion, the water was still in motion).

Creating the Notebook Page

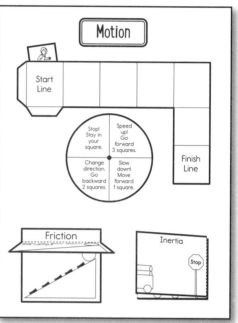

Guide students through the following steps to complete the right-hand page in their notebooks.

1. Add a Table of Contents entry for the Motion pages.

2. Cut out the title and glue it to the top of the page.

3. Cut out the game board. Apply glue to the back of all sections except for the *Start Line* section and attach it below the title. Apply glue to the back of the tabs to create a pocket for the game piece.

4. Cut out the circle. Glue it below the game board. Use a sharpened pencil and a paper clip to create a spinner.

5. Place the runner on the Start Line. Spin the paper clip. Follow the directions to show what type of motion the runner should perform. Play until you reach the Finish Line. Discuss the various types of motion the runner performs. Store the runner in the pocket when not playing.

6. Cut out the ramp piece and glue it to the bottom left of the page. Cut out the *Friction* flap. Apply glue to the back of the top section and attach the flap over the ramp piece.

7. On the ramp under the flap, draw a way to create more friction on the ramp.

8. Cut out the *Inertia* accordion fold. Fold on the dashed lines, alternating the fold direction so that the *Inertia* section is on top. Apply glue to the back of the last section and attach it to the bottom right of the page.

9. Look at the first two frames as the wagon filled with logs approaches a stop sign. In the last frame, add an arrow to show what would happen to the logs if the wagon were to stop suddenly.

Reflect on Learning

To complete the left-hand page, have students create a list of different kinds of motions.

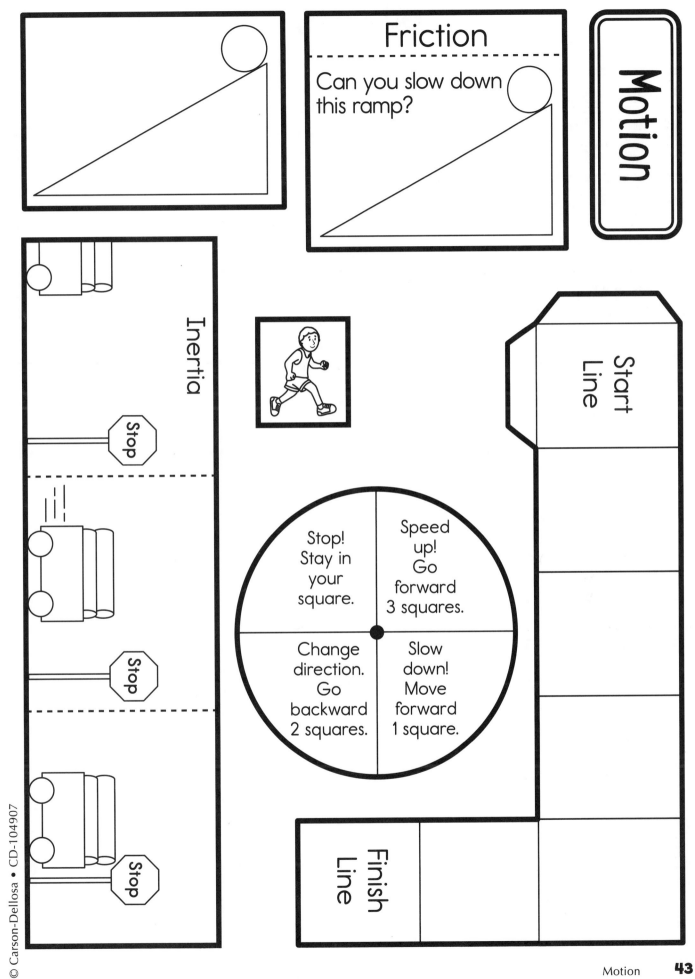

Friction

Can you slow down this ramp?

Motion

Inertia

Stop

Stop

Stop

Start Line

Stop! Stay in your square.

Speed up! Go forward 3 squares.

Change direction. Go backward 2 squares.

Slow down! Move forward 1 square.

Finish Line

Gravity

Introduction

Hold up a pencil and ask the class what will happen when you let go of it. Demonstrate. Discuss why this happens.

Creating the Notebook Page

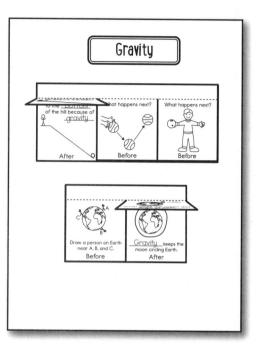

Guide students through the following steps to complete the right-hand page in their notebooks.

1. Add a Table of Contents entry for the Gravity pages.

2. Cut out the title and glue it to the top of the page.

3. Cut out the three-part *Before* flap book and the three-part *After* piece. Cut on the solid lines to create three flaps on the *Before* flap book. Apply glue to the gray glue section on the *After* piece and place the *Before* flap book on top to create a stacked flap book. Glue the flap book below the title.

4. Repeat step 3 with the two-part *After* piece and the two-part *Before* flap book.

5. Read the question or follow the directions on each flap. On the picture under the flap, draw what will happen next and fill in the blanks. (To the **bottom** because of **gravity**; What goes up must come **down**. Gravity pulls objects toward Earth's **core** (or **center**). **Gravity** keeps the moon circling Earth.)

Reflect on Learning

To complete the left-hand page, have students brainstorm examples of when gravity is not a good thing. Have them choose one example and write a story or draw a comic strip to show what happens.

Where will the ball go after it is kicked?

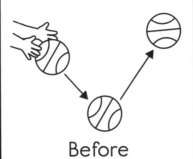

Before

What happens next?

Before

What happens next?

Before

Gravity

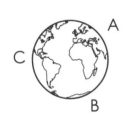

Draw a person on Earth near A, B, and C.

Before

○ moon

What does the moon do? Draw its path.

Before

glue

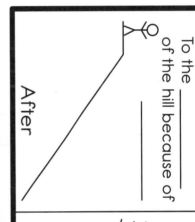

To the _____ of the hill because of _____

After

What goes up must come _____

After

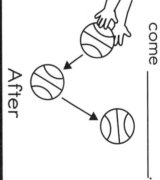

After

glue

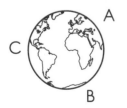

Gravity pulls objects toward Earth's _____.

After

○ moon

_____ keeps the moon circling Earth.

After

After

Magnets

Introduction

Ask students where they see magnets in their everyday lives. Divide students into groups and give each group a magnet (a refrigerator magnet will work). Have them explore the classroom to find objects that are magnetic. Then, have groups share their findings and record their answers on the board. Discuss the property that is true of all of the magnetic items. (They are metal.)

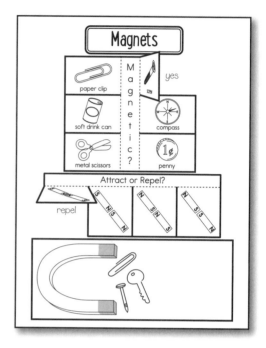

Creating the Notebook Page

Guide students through the following steps to complete the right-hand page in their notebooks.

1. Add a Table of Contents entry for the Magnets pages.

2. Cut out the title and glue it to the top of the page.

3. Cut out the *Magnetic?* flap book. Cut on the solid lines to create six flaps. Apply glue to the back of the middle section and attach it below the title.

4. Under each flap, write *yes* or *no,* depending on whether the object is or is not magnetic.

5. Cut out the *Attract or Repel?* flap book. Cut on the solid lines to create four flaps. Apply glue to the back of the top section and attach it below the *Magnetic?* book.

6. Look at the four pictures. Under each flap, write *attract* or *repel* to describe how the magnets would act in each situation.

7. Cut out the horseshoe magnet piece and glue it to the bottom of the page.

8. On it, draw objects that would be attracted to a magnet.

Reflect on Learning

To complete the left-hand page, have students trace one of their hands. In each finger, have them write one fact about magnets.

Answer Key
paper clip: yes; soft drink can: no; metal scissors: yes; screw: yes; compass: yes; penny: no; NN: repel; NS: attract; SN: attract; SS: repel

Magnets

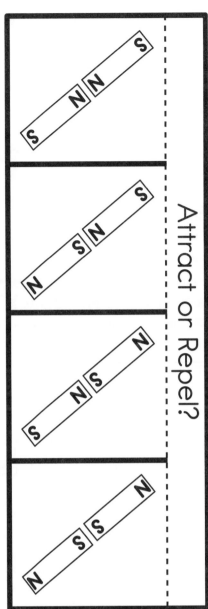

Attract or Repel?

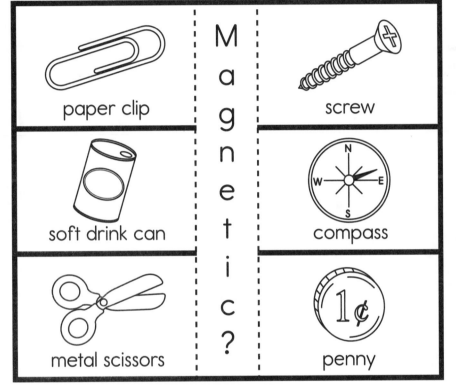

	Magnetic?	
paper clip		screw
soft drink can		compass
metal scissors		penny

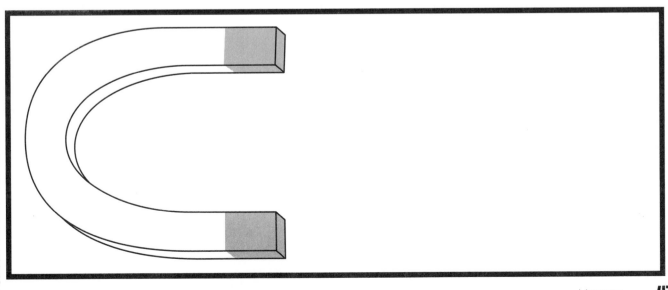

Simple Machines

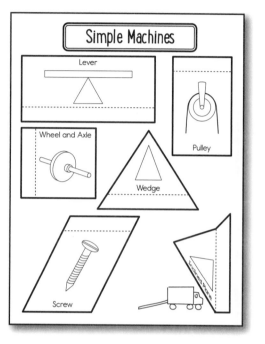

Introduction

Write the name of each simple machine on an index card: lever, pulley, wheel and axle, wedge, screw, and inclined plane. Ask students to name the six main types of simple machines. Write them on the board. Have a volunteer choose an index card and act out or draw on the board an example of that type of simple machine. Have the rest of the class guess which type of simple machine is being portrayed. Repeat with the other index cards.

Creating the Notebook Page

Guide students through the following steps to complete the right-hand page in their notebooks.

1. Add a Table of Contents entry for the Simple Machines pages.

2. Cut out the title and glue it to the top of the page.

3. Cut out the six simple machine flaps.

4. Apply glue to the back of the narrow section of each flap and attach them to the page. It may be helpful to arrange all of the flaps on the page to find an arrangement that fits before gluing any flaps to the page.

5. Under each flap, describe how that simple machine makes work easier. Then, list or draw a picture of something from the real world that uses that kind of simple machine.

Reflect on Learning

To complete the left-hand page, invent and draw something that can complete a task that is made up of more than one simple machine. Label the simple machines.

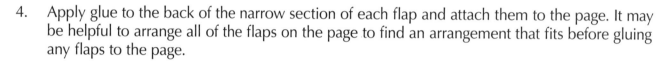

Simple Machines

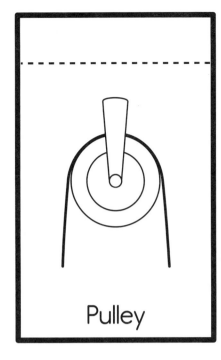

Pulley

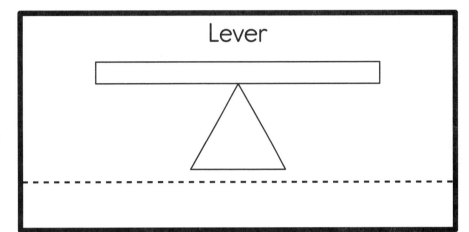

Lever

Wheel and Axle

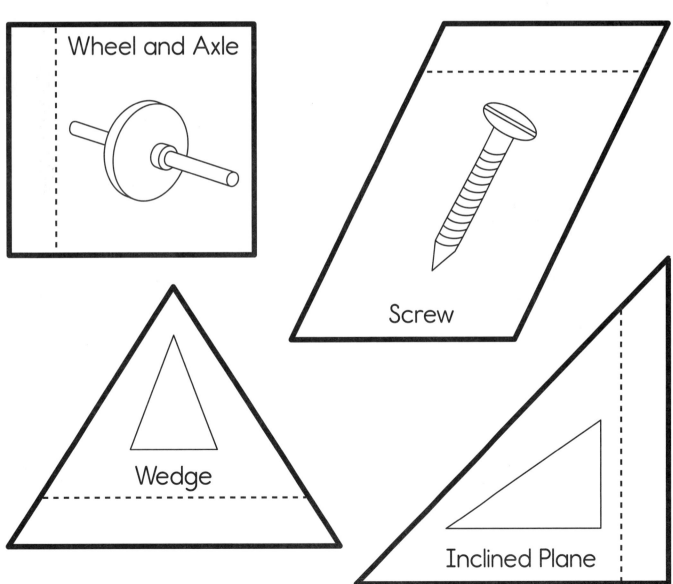

Screw

Wedge

Inclined Plane

Energy

Introduction

Have students turn to partners and share something active they like to do. Ask students where they get their energy to do these activities (food). Ask where plants get their energy (the sun). Discuss how energy comes in many forms, such as heat, light, and sound.

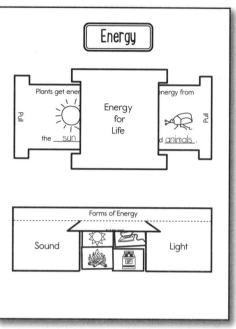

Creating the Notebook Page

Guide students through the following steps to complete the right-hand page in their notebooks.

1. Add a Table of Contents entry for the Energy pages.

2. Cut out the title and glue it to the top of the page.

3. Cut out the *Plants get energy from* slider.

4. Fill in the blanks to tell how plants and animals get energy. (Plants get energy from the **sun**. Animals get energy from **plants** and **animals**.) Then, draw a picture of their energy sources. Place the slider on the page below the title, but do not glue it down.

5. Cut out the *Energy for Life* piece. Apply glue to the back of the top and bottom sections and attach it to the page over the slider so that the slider moves back and forth behind the center section.

6. Cut out the *Forms of Energy* flap book. Cut on the solid lines to create three flaps. Apply glue to the back of the top section and attach it to the page.

7. Cut out the small pictures. Sort and glue each picture under the correct flap. Some may work for more than one flap. If so, make a note or draw it under the other flap.

Reflect on Learning

To complete the left-hand page, have students create a three-column chart with the labels *Heat*, *Light*, and *Sound*. Have them list or cut out and glue examples of each from magazines that are different from those featured on the right-hand page.

Answer Key
Answers will vary but may include: Sound, horn, bell, drums; Heat: stove, campfire, lamp, iron, sun; Light: campfire, lamp, sun, lightning

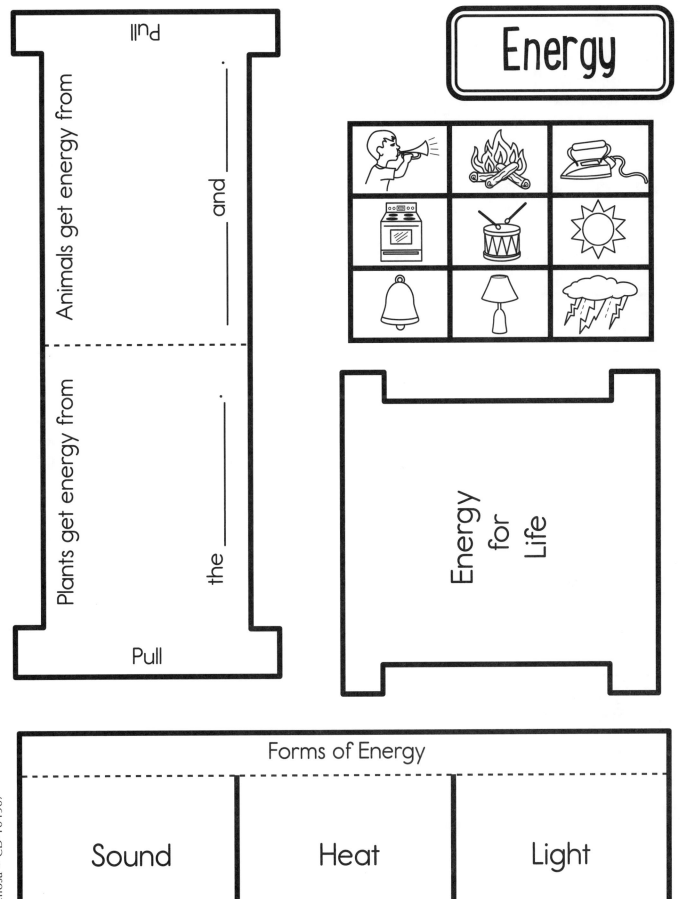

Pull

Animals get energy from

and _____ .

- - - - - - - - - - - -

Plants get energy from

the _____ .

Pull

Energy
for
Life

Forms of Energy

- -

| Sound | Heat | Light |

Heat Energy

Introduction

Review the forms of energy. Ask for examples of heat, or thermal, energy (the sun, a fire, an oven). Distribute a small marshmallow or chocolate square to each student. In groups, have them brainstorm ways to heat the marshmallow or melt the chocolate. On the board, write the words *Ways to Generate Heat*. List students' ideas.

Caution: Before beginning any food activity, ask families' permission and inquire about students' food allergies and religious or other food restrictions.

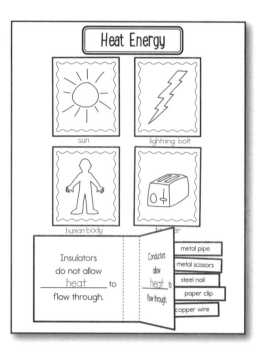

Creating the Notebook Page

Guide students through the following steps to complete the right-hand page in their notebooks.

1. Add a Table of Contents entry for the Heat Energy pages.

2. Cut out the title and glue it to the top of the page.

3. Cut out the four picture frames. Glue them in a 2 by 2 arrangement below the title.

4. In each frame, draw an example of something that creates heat or thermal energy. Label the drawings.

5. Cut out the *Insulators* and *Conductors* flap book. Apply glue to the back of the center section and attach it to the bottom of the page.

6. Fill in the blanks on the flaps to complete the definitions of insulators and conductors. (Insulators do not allow **heat** to flow through. Conductors allow **heat** to flow through.)

7. Cut out the 12 object names. Glue each under the correct flap.

Reflect on Learning

To complete the left-hand page, have students describe a way to keep a slice of pizza warm. Students should explain how insulators or conductors were part of their design.

Answer Key
Insulators: pot holder, wooden spoon, rubber eraser, cotton blanket, candle wax, wool mittens, cork; Conductors: metal pipe, paper clip, metal scissors, copper wire, steel nail

Heat Energy

pot holder
wooden spoon
metal pipe
paper clip
rubber eraser
metal scissors
cotton blanket
candle wax
copper wire
wool mittens
steel nail
cork

Insulators
do not allow
_____ to
flow through.

Conductors
allow
_____ to
flow through.

Sound

Introduction

Bang on a table or a desk. Ask students what kind of energy you are producing (sound). Ask them for ways we can categorize sound (loudness and pitch). Give each student four self-stick notes. Have students write one of the following on each: *high pitch*, *low pitch*, *loud sound*, and *soft sound*. Have students walk around the classroom to look for objects that make each type of sound. They may tap on surfaces and use pencils as mallets. When they find the desired objects, have students leave the matching self-stick notes on them. Have students observe all of the different kinds of sounds in the classroom.

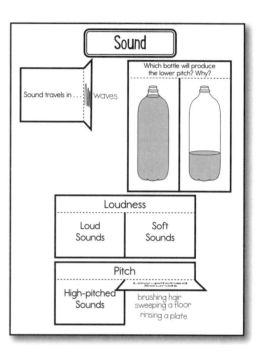

Creating the Notebook Page

Guide students through the following steps to complete the right-hand page in their notebooks.

1. Add a Table of Contents entry for the Sound pages.

2. Cut out the title and glue it to the top of the page.

3. Cut out the *Sound travels in* flap. Apply glue to the back of the left section and attach it below and to the left of the title.

4. Under the flap, complete the sentence (Sound travels in . . . **waves, through material**).

5. Cut out the *Which bottle will* flap book. Cut on the solid line to create two flaps. Apply glue to the back of the top section and attach it below and to the right of the title.

6. Cut out the two *This bottle will* answer pieces. Read the question on the flap and the two answers. Glue each answer under the correct flap. Complete each sentence. (Under the left flap: This bottle will produce the higher pitch because it has a **smaller** amount of air, making a higher sound. Under the right flap: This bottle will produce the lower pitch because it has a a **larger** amount of air, making a lower sound.)

7. Cut out the *Loudness* and *Pitch* flap books. Cut on the solid lines to create two flaps on each. Apply glue to the back of the top sections and attach them to the page.

8. Under the *Loudness* flaps, write examples of loud sounds and soft sounds. Under the *Pitch* flaps, write examples of high-pitched sounds and low-pitched sounds.

Reflect on Learning

To complete the left-hand page, have students name a sound that is loud and low and name a sound that is soft and high.

Which bottle will produce the lower pitch? Why?

Sound

This bottle will produce the lower pitch because it has a _____ amount of air, making a lower sound.

This bottle will produce the higher pitch because it has a _____ amount of air, making a higher sound.

Loudness

| Loud Sounds | Soft Sounds |

Pitch

| High-pitched Sounds | Low-pitched Sounds |

Sound travels in . . . .

© Carson-Dellosa • CD-104907

Sound   **55**

Light

Introduction

Bring in a flashlight or provide one for each group. In a dark room, demonstrate how light travels in a straight line. Have students brainstorm and try different ways to change the light's path, such as with a mirror or an opaque surface. Then, demonstrate how a pencil is refracted in a clear glass of water.

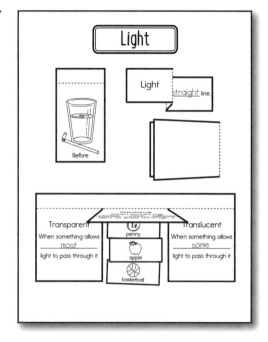

Creating the Notebook Page

Guide students through the following steps to complete the right-hand page in their notebooks.

1. Add a Table of Contents entry for the Light pages.

2. Cut out the title and glue it to the top of the page.

3. Cut out the *Before and After* flaps. Apply glue to the gray glue section and place the *Before* flap on top to create a stacked two-flap book. Glue it below and to the left of the title.

4. Look at the top picture, which shows a straw before it is placed into a glass of water. The *After* picture shows what the straw would look like if placed into the glass of water. Discuss how the straw appears bent due to the way light refracts in water.

5. Cut out the *Light* accordion fold. Fold on the dashed lines, alternating the fold direction so that the word *Light* is on top. Apply glue to the back of the last section and attach it below and to the right of the title. Fill in the blank to complete the sentence. (Light travels in a **straight** line.)

6. Cut out the *Reflection* flap. Fold on the dashed line. Apply glue to the back of the left section and attach it below the *Light* accordion fold. Fill in the blank to complete the sentence. (Reflection is when light **rays** bounce off a surface.) On the underside of the flap, write an example of a place or instance you might see a reflection.

7. Cut out the *Transparent, Opaque, Translucent* flap book. Cut on the solid lines to create three flaps. Apply glue to back of the top section and attach it to the bottom of the page. Fill in the missing words on the flaps. (When something allows **all** light to pass through it. When something **does not allow** light to pass through it. When something allows **some** light to pass through it.)

8. Cut out the nine objects. Read each label and glue it under the correct flap.

Reflect on Learning

To complete the left-hand page, have students choose a room in their houses and list the objects that are translucent, transparent, and opaque.

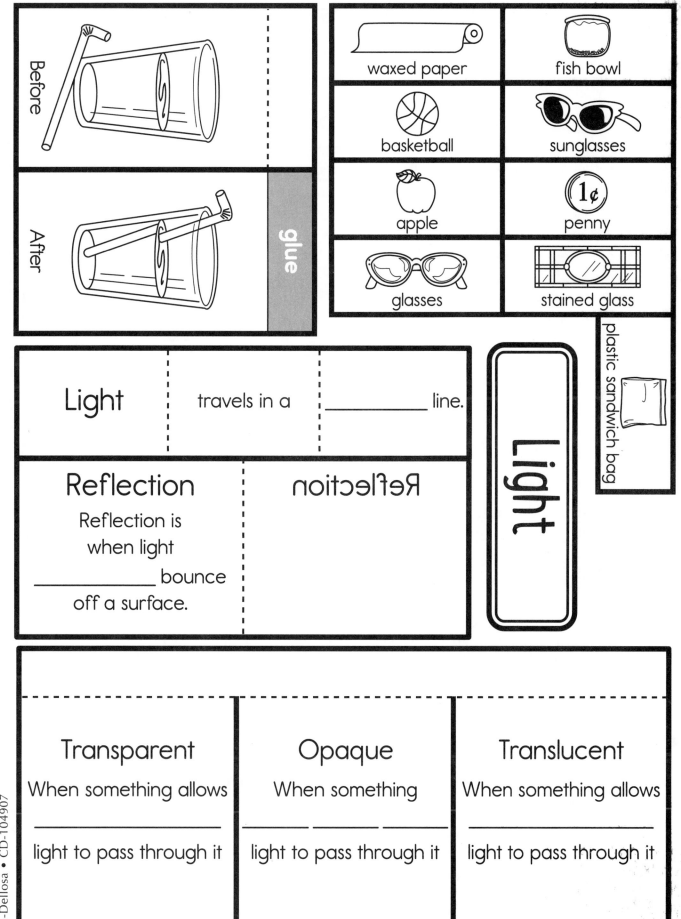

Before

After

glue

waxed paper

fish bowl

basketball

sunglasses

apple

penny

glasses

stained glass

plastic sandwich bag

Light : travels in a _____ line.

Reflection : Reflection

Reflection is
when light
_____ bounce
off a surface.

Light

Transparent

When something allows

_____

light to pass through it

Opaque

When something

_____

light to pass through it

Translucent

When something allows

_____

light to pass through it

Earth's Resources

Introduction

Ask students what it means if something is man-made. Ask what the opposite of man-made would be (natural). Distribut self-stick notes so that each student gets two. Have them write *natural* on one and *man-made* on the other. Have students label things in the classroom that are natural and man-made with their self-stick notes. Discuss as a class any that are debatable.

Creating the Notebook Page

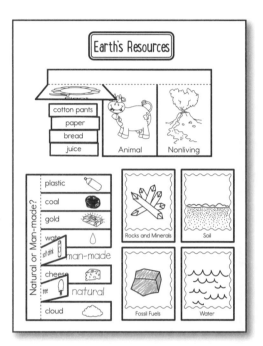

Guide students through the following steps to complete the right-hand page in their notebooks.

1. Add a Table of Contents entry for the Earth's Resources pages.

2. Cut out the title and glue it to the top of the page.

3. Cut out the *Plant, Animal, Nonliving* flap book. Cut on the solid lines to create three flaps. Apply glue to the back of the top section and attach it below the title.

4. Cut out the 12 word strips. Sort them according to which resource they came from: plant, animal, or nonliving. Glue them under the correct flaps.

5. Cut out the *Natural or Man-Made?* flap book. Cut on the solid lines to create eight flaps. Apply glue to the back of the left section and attach it to the left side of the page.

6. Under each flap, write whether the object is natural or man-made.

7. Cut out the four picture frames. Glue them to the right side of the page.

8. Draw a picture in each frame to illustrate each type of natural resource. If desired, add a caption to each.

Reflect on Learning

To complete the left-hand page, have students create a T-chart labeled *Natural* and *Man-Made*. Have students cut out pictures from magazines and glue them under the correct headings.

Answer Key
Plants: bread, paper, juice, cotton pants; Animals: milk, wool sweater, yogurt, eggs; Nonliving: baby powder, diamond, concrete, glass

| Plant | Animal | Nonliving |

bread	baby powder	yogurt	cotton pants
milk	juice	eggs	concrete
paper	wool sweater	diamond	glass

Natural or Man-made?

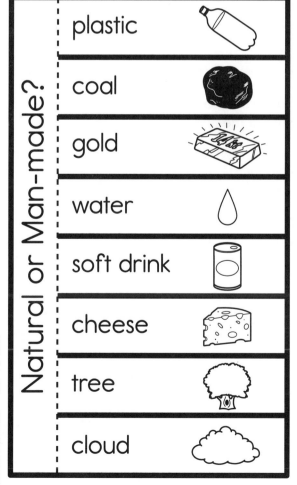

- plastic
- coal
- gold
- water
- soft drink
- cheese
- tree
- cloud

Rocks and Minerals

Soil

Fossil Fuels

Water

Rocks

Introduction

Bring rocks to class or have students bring rocks to class to share. Divide the class into small groups. Make sure you have enough rocks for each group to have one to view. Tape a number on each rock with masking tape. Discuss where rocks come from. Allow students to view the rocks up close. If possible, distribute hand lenses. Have students record the rock numbers and list adjectives to describe each rock. Afterward, have a student in each group read a description of their rock and have the rest of the class guess which rock (by number) he is describing.

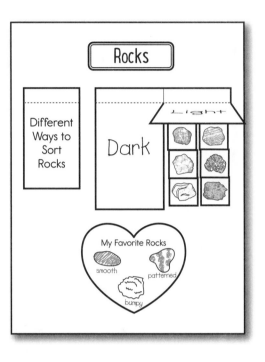

Creating the Notebook Page

Guide students through the following steps to complete the right-hand page in their notebooks.

1. Add a Table of Contents entry for the Rocks pages.

2. Cut out the title and glue it to the top of the page.

3. Cut out the *Different Ways to Sort Rocks* flap. Apply glue to the back of the top section and attach it below and to the left of the title.

4. Under the flap, list different ways to sort rocks such as *color*.

5. Cut out the blank flap book. Cut on the solid line to create two flaps. Apply glue to the back of the top section and attach it below and to the right of the title.

6. Cut out the 12 rocks. Choose a way to sort the rocks into two categories such as *smooth* and *bumpy* or *dark* and *light*. Write the two categories on the flaps. Sort and glue the rocks under the correct flaps. If a rock does not fit either category, glue it next to the page's title.

7. Cut out the *My Favorite Rocks* heart. Glue it to the bottom of the page. Draw three of your favorite rocks and label them. If desired, describe the properties of each rock.

Reflect on Learning

To complete the left-hand page, have students describe how describing and sorting rocks by properties can be useful to scientists who study rocks.

Rocks

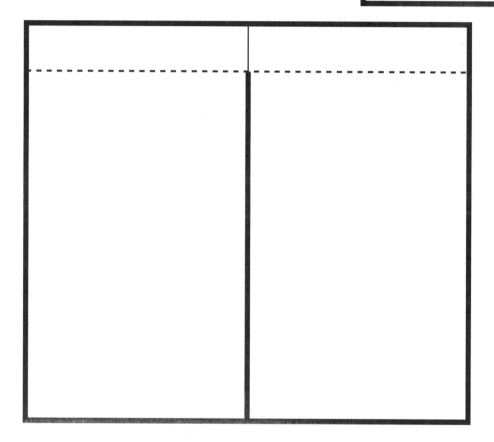

My Favorite Rocks

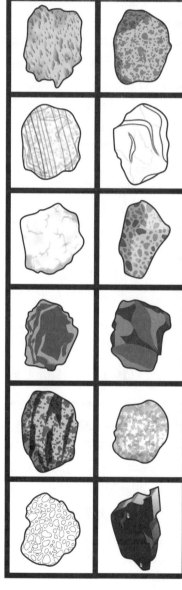

Landforms

Introduction

Post a physical map of your state on the wall or distribute maps to small groups. Have students identify the landforms they see. List the landforms on the board. Discuss the differences between the landforms.

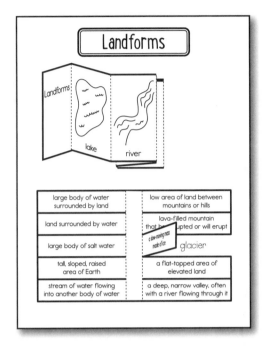

Creating the Notebook Page

Guide students through the following steps to complete the right-hand page in their notebooks.

1. Add a Table of Contents entry for the Landforms pages.

2. Cut out the title and glue it to the top of the page.

3. Cut out the *Landforms* accordion fold. Fold on the dashed lines, alternating the fold direction so that the word *Landforms* is on top. Apply glue to the gray glue section and attach it below the title.

4. On the bottom of the back of each section, write a word: *glacier, island, volcano, mountain, valley,* or *ocean* in order to create a double-sided book with a cover and 10 pages. For each labeled section, draw a picture of the landform.

5. Cut out the flap book. Cut on the solid lines to create 10 flaps. Apply glue to the back of the middle section and attach it to the bottom of the page.

6. Read each definition. Under each flap, write the name of the landform that the definition describes.

Reflect on Learning

To complete the left-hand page, have students write a riddle for three landforms. Have them write the answers upside down at the bottom of the page. Allow students to exchange notebooks with a partner and solve their partners's riddles.

Answer Key
large body of water surrounded by land: lake; land surrounded by water: island; large body of salt water: ocean; tall, sloped raised area of Earth: mountain; body of water flowing into another body of water: river; low area of land between mountains or hills: valley; lava-filled mountain that has erupted or will erupt: volcano; a slow-moving mass made of ice: glacier; a flat-topped area of elevated land: plateau; a deep, narrow valley, often with a river flowing through it: canyon

Landforms

Landforms	lake	river	plateau	canyon

glue

large body of water surrounded by land

land surrounded by water

large body of salt water

tall, sloped, raised area of Earth

stream of water flowing into another body of water

low area of land between mountains or hills

lava-filled mountain that has erupted or will erupt

a slow-moving mass made of ice

a flat-topped area of elevated land

a deep, narrow valley, often with a river flowing through it

Changes to Earth's Surface

Each student will need a brass paper fastener to complete this page.

Introduction

Distribute a cookie or sugar cube to each student or group, as well as a small container with a lid such as a plastic food container. Explain that the cookie will represent a boulder. Ask students what will happen if you put the object in the container and shake the container. Have students try it. Explain that this process is similar to weathering. List the different types of weathering on the board. Ask students to demonstrate erosion with their cookies. (Students should brush or blow the crumbs away from the cookie.)

Caution: Before beginning any food activity, ask families' permission and inquire about students' food allergies and religious or other food restrictions.

Creating the Notebook Page

Guide students through the following steps to complete the right-hand page in their notebooks.

1. Add a Table of Contents entry for the Changes to Earth's Surface pages.

2. Cut out the title and glue it to the top of the page.

3. Cut out the *Slow Processes* and *Rapid Processes* flap book. Cut on the solid line to create two flaps. Apply glue to the back of the top section and attach it below the title.

4. Cut out the seven word strips. Read each word and think about what it means. Glue each under the correct flap.

5. Cut out the circle and the *Types of Weathering* piece. On the circle, draw and label four types of weathering.

6. Place the *Types of Weathering* piece on top of the four-section circle. Push a brass paper fastener through the center dots of the two pieces to attach them. It may be helpful to create the hole in each piece separately first. Apply glue to the back of the top piece's tabs and attach it to the bottom of the page. The brass paper fastener should not go through the page, and the circle beneath should spin freely. Share your weathering wheel with a partner.

Reflect on Learning

To complete the left-hand page, have students draw a comic strip of a landform affected by weathering.

Answer Key
Slow Processes: erosion, weathering, deposition; Rapid Processes: erosion, landslide, earthquake, volcano, storm (Note: Erosion and volcanoes can fit under either category.)

64

Changes to Earth's Surface

erosion
landslide
earthquake
volcano
storm
weathering
deposition

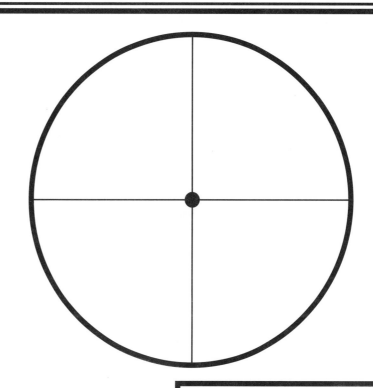

Types

of

Weathering

Slow
Processes

Rapid
Processes

Sources of Energy

Introduction

Discuss with the class what energy source lights and computers use, as well as the energy source a gas stove uses. Divide the class into small groups and have each make a list of other sources of energy. Have groups share their lists. If another group also has a particular source, have them all cross it out. Check to see which group has the most original sources left.

Creating the Notebook Page

Guide students through the following steps to complete the right-hand page in their notebooks.

1. Add a Table of Contents entry for the Sources of Energy pages.

2. Cut out the title and glue it to the top of the page.

3. Cut out the *Natural Sources of Energy* hexagon. Apply glue to the back of the center section and attach it below the title.

4. Cut out the six types of energy strips. Glue each type under the correct flap on the hexagon.

5. Cut out the *Coal can generate* accordion fold. Fold on the dashed lines, alternating the fold direction so that the *Coal can generate* section is on top. Apply glue to the back of the last section and attach it to the bottom center of the page.

6. Fill in the blanks to complete the sentences. (Coal can generate **electricity**, which can be used for **powering appliances and light**. Oil or petroleum can be refined into **gasoline**, which is used to pwer **vehicles**. Natural gas is used in **homes** to power **ovens, furnaces, and stoves**. Note: Items each energy source is used for may vary.)

7. Cut out the *Renewable* and *Nonrenewable* flaps. Apply glue to the back of the top sections and attach them to the bottom of the page on either side of the accordion fold.

8. On the front of the flaps, complete the definitions for renewable and nonrenewable energy sources. (Renewable energy sources are sources that **can be replenished**. Nonrenewable energy sources are sources that **cannot be replenished**.) Under each flap, give examples of energy sources that fit the category.

Reflect on Learning

To complete the left-hand page, have students draw a picture that shows three different sources of natural energy. Have them label the energy sources.

© Carson-Dellosa • CD-104907

Sources of Energy

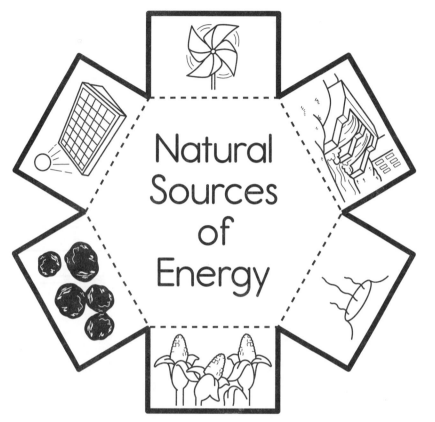

Natural Sources of Energy

water (hydroelectric power)	wind	coal (fossil fuel)
plants and animals (biofuels)	the earth (geothermal power)	the sun (solar energy)

Renewable energy sources are sources that _____ _____ _____.

Nonrenewable energy sources are sources that _____ _____ _____.

Coal can generate	_____, which can be used for	_____.
Oil or petroleum can be refined into	_____, which is used to power	_____.
Natural gas is used in	_____ to power	_____.

The Solar System

Introduction

Write the names of the eight planets on index cards so that you have one card for each student. Have students name the eight planets. Write them on the board. Distribute the index cards so that each student gets one. Ask questions about the planets, such as *Which planets have rings?* Students whose planets have rings should stand and hold up their index cards.

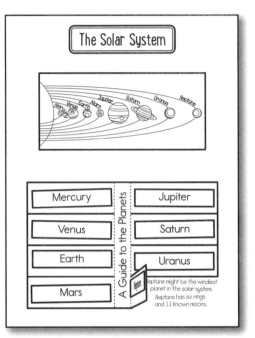

Creating the Notebook Page

Guide students through the following steps to complete the right-hand page in their notebooks.

1. Add a Table of Contents entry for The Solar System pages.

2. Cut out the title and glue it to the top of the page.

3. Cut out the piece with the sun and the planets. Glue it on the page below the title.

4. Cut out the names of the planets. Use them to help you name the planets in the correct order on the picture. (Note: The planets' sizes and distances from the sun are not drawn to scale.) Write the correct name on the orbit line above each planet.

5. Cut out the flap book. Cut on the solid lines to create eight flaps. Apply glue to the back of the center section and attach it to the bottom of the page.

6. Glue the names of the planets onto the fronts of the flaps in the order they are from the sun.

7. Under each flap, write facts about the planet.

Reflect on Learning

To complete the left-hand page, have students choose one planet to write a poem about. Poems should include facts about the planet.

Answer Key
1. Mercury, 2. Venus, 3. Earth, 4. Mars, 5. Jupiter, 6. Saturn, 7. Uranus, 8. Neptune

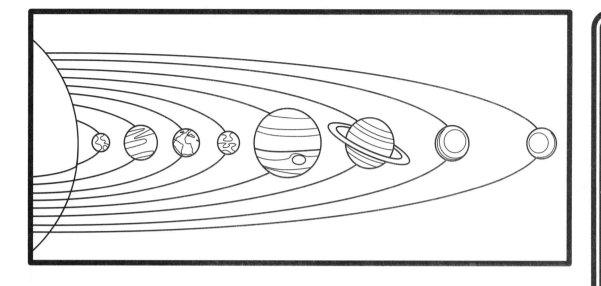

The Solar System

A Guide to the Planets

Earth	Mars	Mercury	Jupiter
Saturn	Neptune	Uranus	Venus

The Moon and Earth

Each student will need a brass paper fastener to complete this page.

Introduction

Discuss moon phases with students. To demonstrate why the moon has phases, have one student use a ball to represent the moon, another student stand to represent Earth, and a third student hold a flashlight to represent the sun. As the student with the ball moves around the student representing Earth, it will show the new moon, first quarter, full moon, and last quarter phases before returning to the new moon phase.

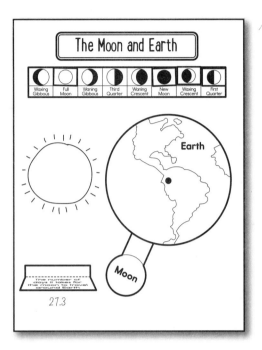

Creating the Notebook Page

Guide students through the following steps to complete the right-hand page in their notebooks.

1. Add a Table of Contents entry for The Moon and Earth pages.

2. Cut out the title and glue it to the top of the page.

3. Cut out the labeled moon phases strip. Glue it below the title.

4. Cut out each missing moon phase. Glue each where it belongs on the moon phases strip.

5. Cut out the *Earth* circle, the *Moon* piece, and the small gray circle. Place the *Earth* circle on top of the moon piece and then place the small gray circle on the bottom with the gray glue side down. Push a brass paper fastener through the dots at the center of the *Earth* piece, the *Moon* piece, and the small gray circle to connect the three pieces. It may be helpful to create the hole in each piece separately first. Apply glue to the gray glue section and attach it below and to the right of the moon phases piece. The brass paper fastener should not go through the page, and the moon should orbit Earth freely.

6. Draw a large sun on the page to the left of the Earth.

7. Choose one of the moon's phases. Move the moon around Earth to show where it is in relation to the sun.

8. Cut out *The number* flap. Apply glue to the back of the top section and attach it to the bottom of the page, to the left of the moon piece.

9. Answer the question under the flap (**about 28**).

Reflect on Learning

To complete the left-hand page, have students write a haiku describing a moon phase.

The Moon and Earth

Waxing Gibbous	Full Moon	Waning Gibbous	Third Quarter	Waning Crescent	New Moon	Waxing Crescent	First Quarter

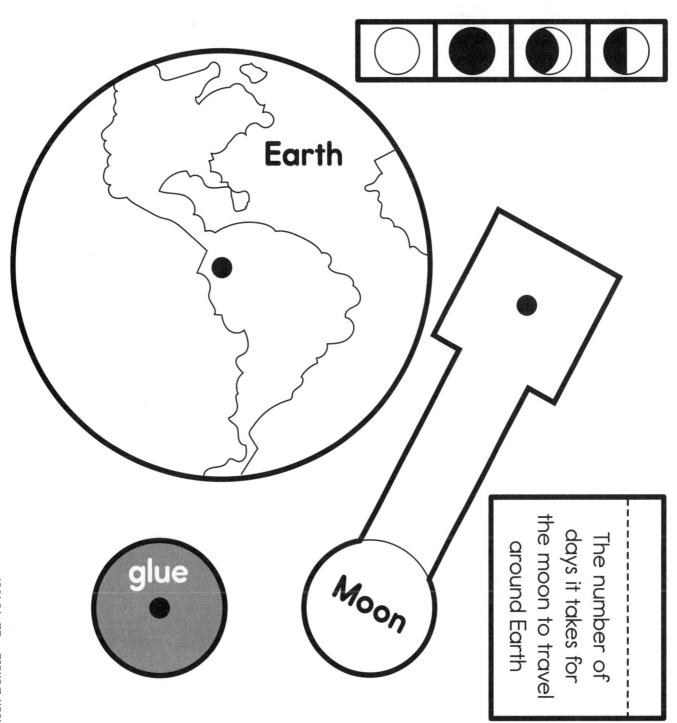

Earth

glue

Moon

The number of days it takes for the moon to travel around Earth

The Sun and Earth

Introduction

Using a globe, have one student come to the front of the room to show what causes day and night. Have another student stand to represent the sun. Challenge the first student to use a globe to show each of the four seasons for your class's location. The student should use the position of Earth and the tilt of its axis in relation to the sun to explain why the hemisphere experiences that season at that time. For example, during winter, the northern hemisphere is tilted away from the sun.

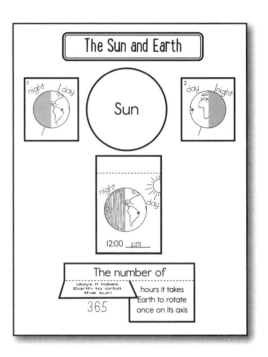

Creating the Notebook Page

Guide students through the following steps to complete the right-hand page in their notebooks.

1. Add a Table of Contents entry for The Sun and Earth pages.

2. Cut out the title and glue it to the top of the page.

3. Cut out the *Sun* circle. Glue it below the title in the center.

4. Cut out the two Earth pieces. Glue *1* to the left of the sun and glue *2* to the right of the sun.

5. Discuss how the rotation of Earth causes night and day. Label *night* and *day* on each piece.

6. Cut out the Earth flaps. Apply glue to the gray glue section and place the other flap on top to create a stacked flap book. Glue it to the middle of the page.

7. For each flap, look at where the dot on Earth is in relation to the sun. Shade each Earth to show which hemisphere is experiencing night, and label both hemispheres of Earth with the words *night* and *day*. Then, fill in the blanks to make the time *am* or *pm*.

8. Cut out *The number of* flap book. Cut on the solid line to create two flaps. Apply glue to the back of the top section and attach it to the bottom center of the page.

9. Under each flap, write the missing number (**365** days; **24** hours).

Reflect on Learning

To complete the left-hand page, have students choose two times of day and draw the relationship between the sun and Earth at each time.

The Sun and Earth

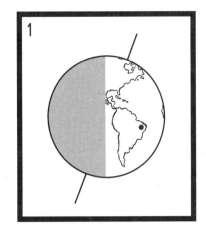

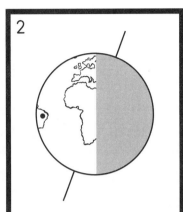

Sun

The number of

| days it takes Earth to orbit the sun | hours it takes Earth to rotate once on its axis |

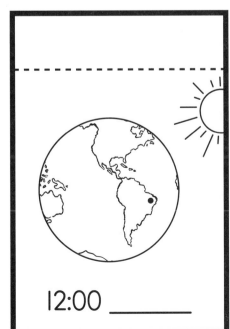

12:00 _____

glue

12:00 _____

Weather and Climate

Introduction

In advance, create a chart on the board with your location's average temperature (°F) and rainfall (inches) by month. Students will use it to complete a graph later. As a class, discuss today's weather. Ask what the climate is like. Discuss the difference between weather and climate.

Creating the Notebook Page

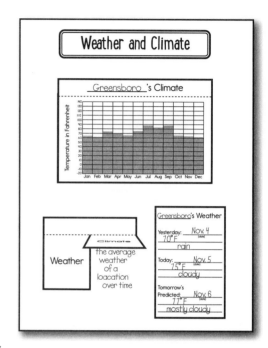

Guide students through the following steps to complete the right-hand page in their notebooks.

1. Add a Table of Contents entry for the Weather and Climate pages.

2. Cut out the title and glue it to the top of the page.

3. Cut out the two graphs. Apply glue to the gray glue section of the *Rainfall* flap and place the *Temperature* flap on top to create a stacked flap book. Glue it below the title.

4. Fill in the blank in the graph's title with your location. Using the information on the board, complete the graphs with the monthly average temperature and rainfall for your region.

5. Cut out the *Weather, Climate* flap book. Cut on the solid line to create two flaps. Apply glue to the back of the top section and attach it to the bottom left of the page.

6. Under the flaps, write definitions of *weather* and *climate*.

7. Cut out the *Weather* piece and glue it to the bottom right of the page.

8. Fill in the blank with your location. Write the date and weather for yesterday and today. Write the predicted weather for tomorrow.

Reflect on Learning

To complete the left-hand page, have students name one location that has a similar climate to theirs and one that has a very different climate. Have them predict the weather for both places six months from now.

Answer Key
weather: the daily conditions such as temperature, precipitation, and wind; climate: the average weather of a location over time

Weather and Climate

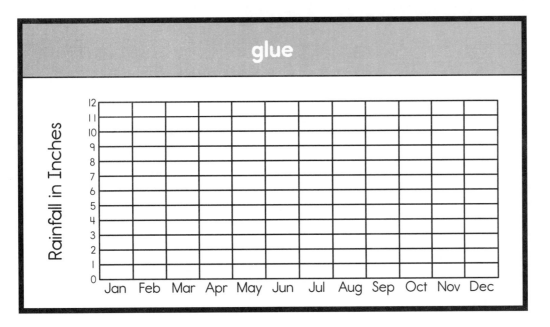

Rainfall in Inches

12
11
10
9
8
7
6
5
4
3
2
1
0

Jan Feb Mar Apr May Jun Jul Aug Sep Oct Nov Dec

_____'s Climate

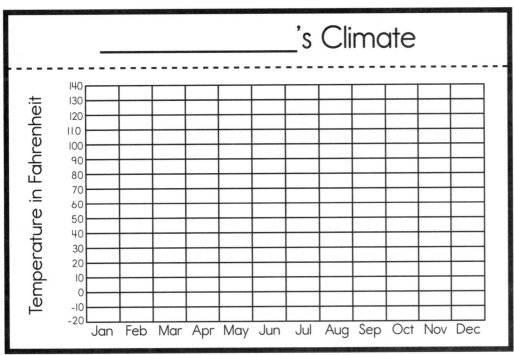

Temperature in Fahrenheit

140
130
120
110
100
90
80
70
60
50
40
30
20
10
0
-10
-20

Jan Feb Mar Apr May Jun Jul Aug Sep Oct Nov Dec

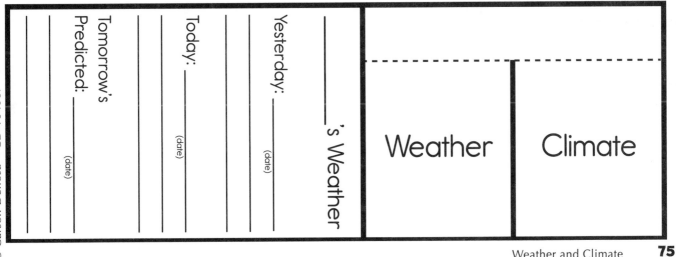

_____'s Weather

Yesterday: _____ (date)

Today: _____ (date)

Tomorrow's
Predicted: _____ (date)

_____

Weather

Climate

Human Impact

Introduction

Display pictures of various items commonly found in the garbage, as well as recyclable materials. Have the class help you sort the items into piles. Let students decide whether items should go in the trash, the recycling bin, or a compost bin. Ask about and discuss ways we help and hurt our planet.

Creating the Notebook Page

Guide students through the following steps to complete the right-hand page in their notebooks.

1. Add a Table of Contents entry for the Human Impact pages.

2. Cut out the title and glue it to the top of the page.

3. Cut out the *How We Can Help* flap book. Cut on the solid lines to create three flaps. Apply glue to the back of the top section and attach it below the title.

4. Under each flap, give examples of things that we can reduce, reuse, or recycle. Brainstorm things that can be found at school, at home, and other places. On top of each flap, draw and label one of the examples written under the flap.

5. Cut out the *Ways We Impact Earth* hexagon. Apply glue to the back of the center section and attach it to the page.

6. On each flap, write and draw something we do that impacts Earth. Under the flap, write the word *help* or *hurt*.

Reflect on Learning

To complete the left-hand page, have students write short letters to the principal that list ways the school can help diminish its footprint on Earth.

How We Can Help

Reduce	Reuse	Recycle

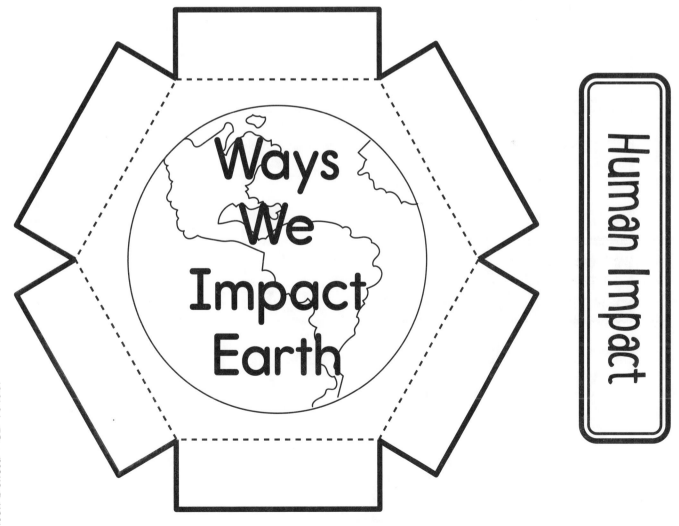

Ways We Impact Earth

Human Impact

Tabs

Cut out each tab and label it. Apply glue to the back of each tab and align it on the outside edge of the page with only the label section showing beyond the edge. Then, fold each tab to seal the page inside.

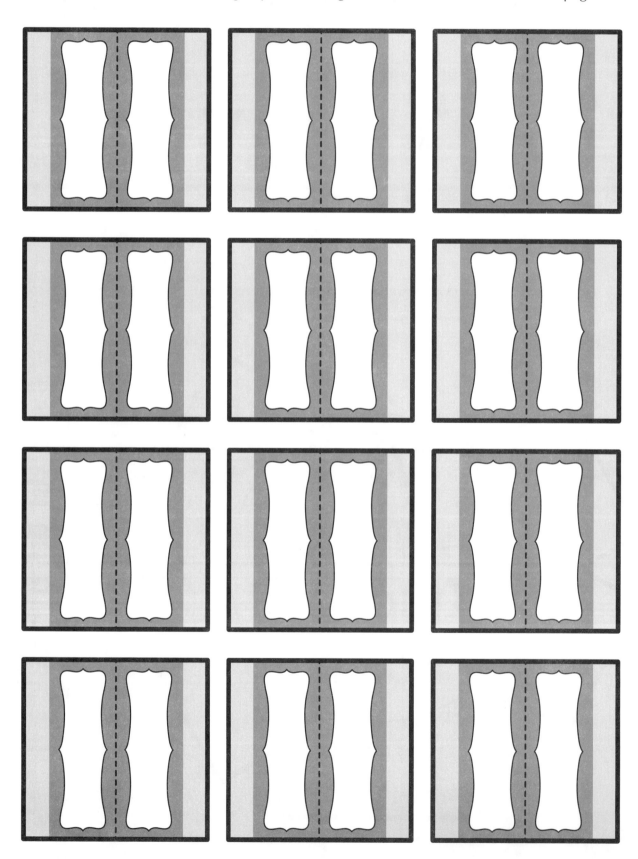

Cut out the KWL chart and cut on the solid lines to create three separate flaps. Apply glue to the back of the Topic section to attach the chart to a notebook page.

Topic: _____

What I

Know

What I

Wonder

What I

Learned

Library Pocket

Cut out the library pocket on the solid lines. Fold in the side tabs and apply glue to them before folding up the front of the pocket. Apply glue to the back of the pocket to attach it to a notebook page.

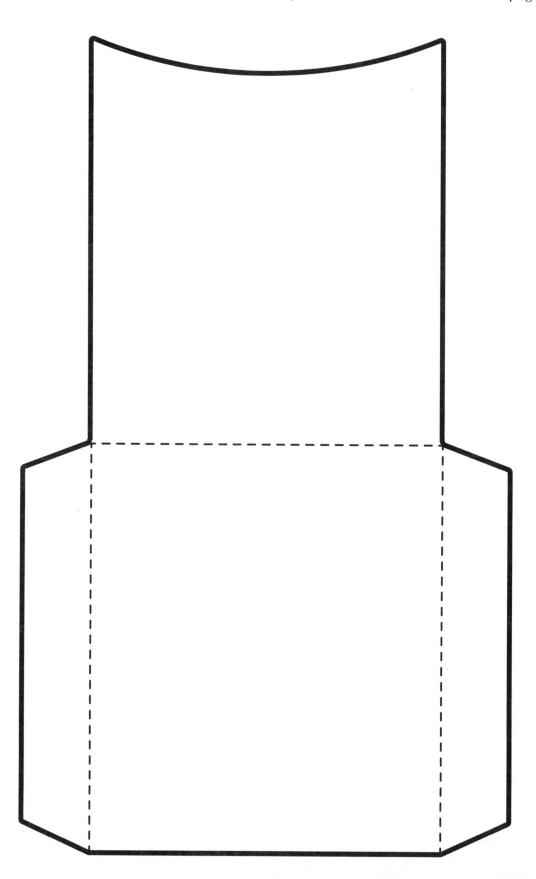

Envelope

Cut out the envelope on the solid lines. Fold in the side tabs and apply glue to them before folding up the rectangular front of the envelope. Fold down the triangular flap to close the envelope. Apply glue to the back of the envelope to attach it to a notebook page.

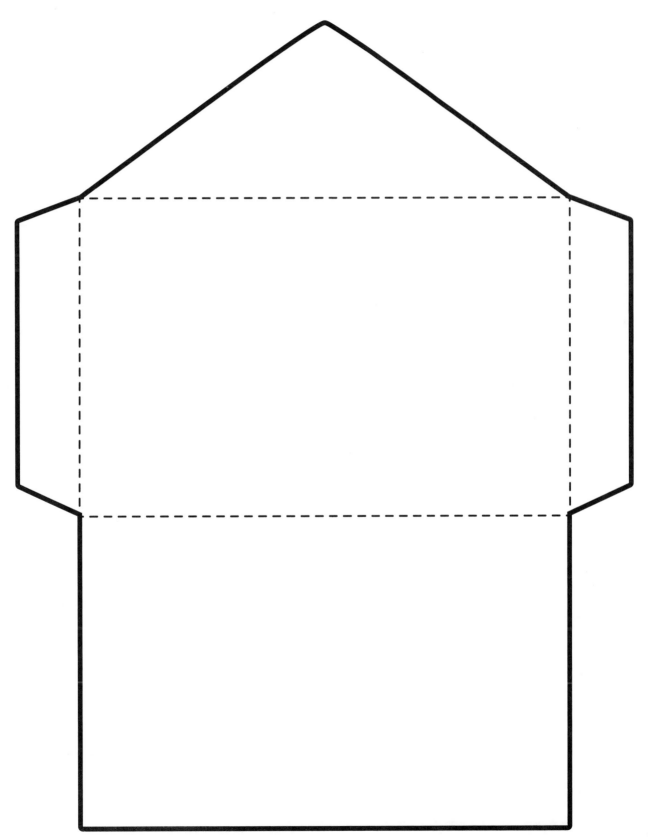

Pocket and Cards

Cut out the pocket on the solid lines. Fold over the front of the pocket. Then, apply glue to the tabs and fold them around the back of the pocket. Apply glue to the back of the pocket to attach it to a notebook page. Cut out the cards and store them in the envelope.

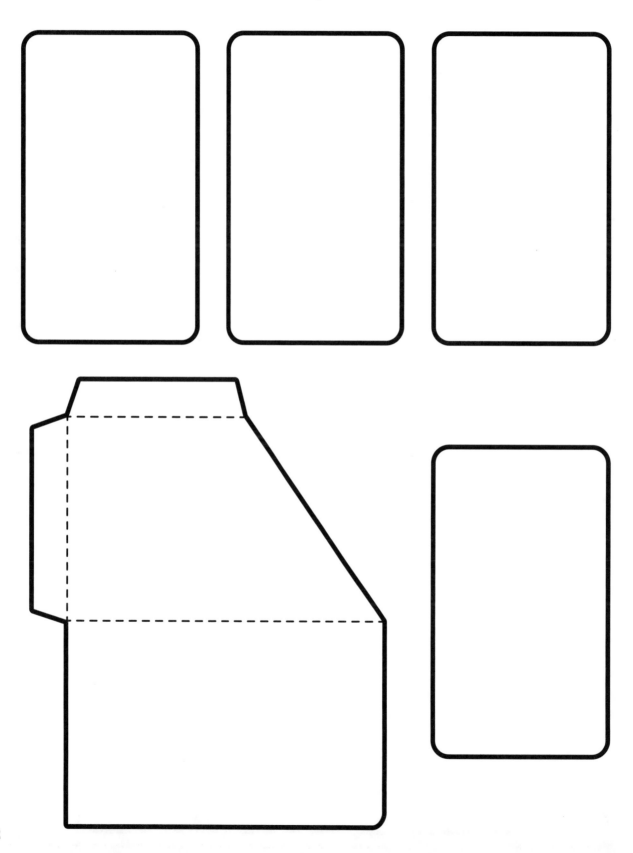

Six-Flap Shutter Fold

Cut out the shutter fold around the outside border. Then, cut on the solid lines to create six flaps. Fold the flaps toward the center. Apply glue to the back of the shutter fold to attach it to a notebook page.

If desired, this template can be modified to create a four-flap shutter fold by cutting off the bottom row. You can also create two three-flap books by cutting it in half down the center line.

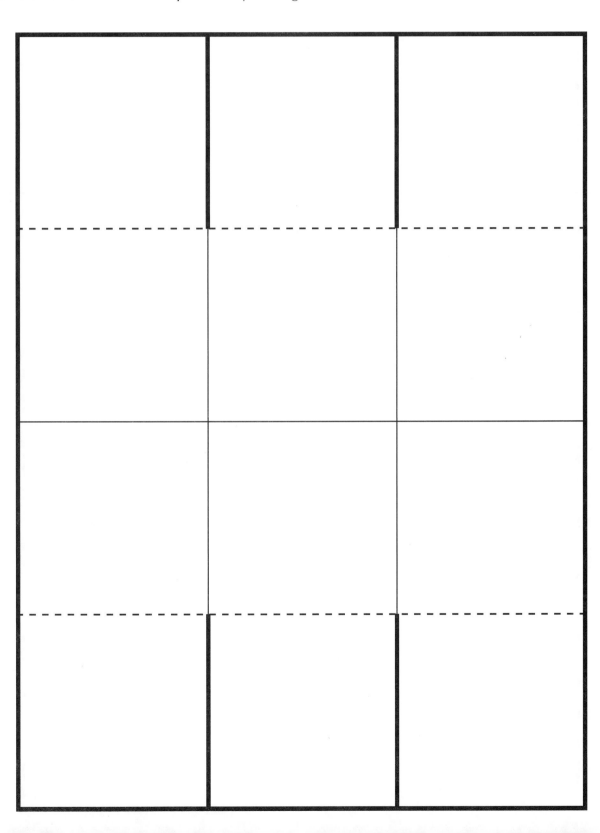

Eight-Flap Shutter Fold

Cut out the shutter fold around the outside border. Then, cut on the solid lines to create eight flaps. Fold the flaps toward the center. Apply glue to the back of the shutter fold to attach it to a notebook page.

If desired, this template can be modified to create two four-flap shutter folds by cutting off the bottom two rows. You can also create two four-flap books by cutting it in half down the center line.

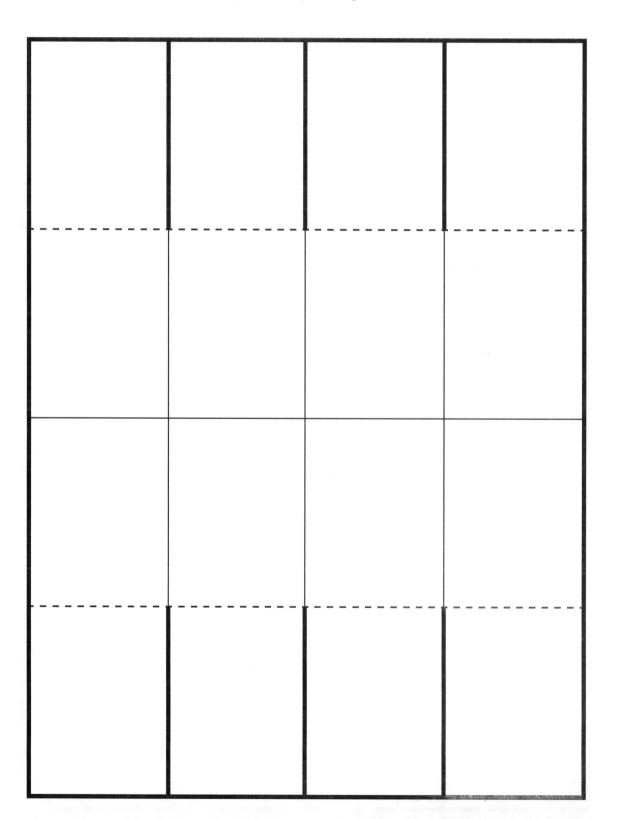

Flap Book—Eight Flaps

Cut out the flap book around the outside border. Then, cut on the solid lines to create eight flaps. Apply glue to the back of the center section to attach it to a notebook page.

If desired, this template can be modified to create a six-flap or two four-flap books by cutting off the bottom row or two. You can also create a tall four-flap book by cutting off the flaps on the left side.

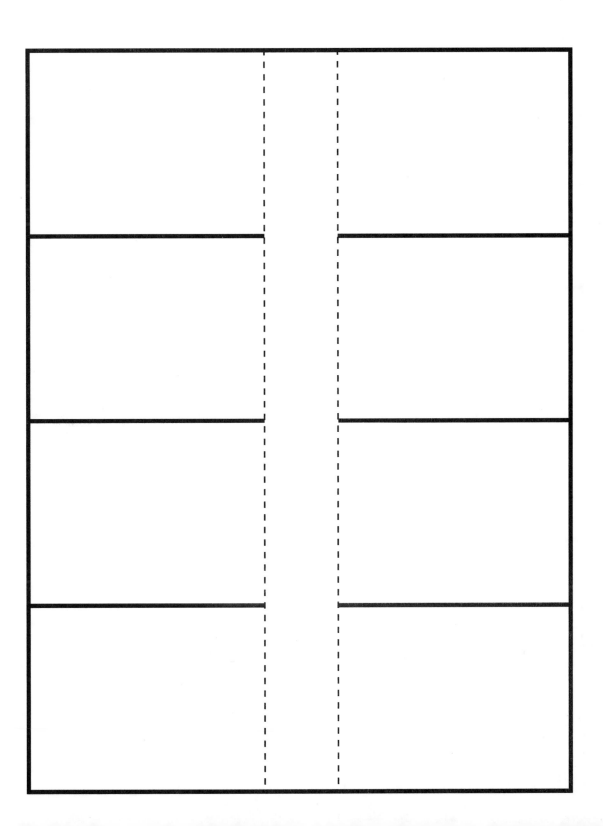

Flap Book—Twelve Flaps

Cut out the flap book around the outside border. Then, cut on the solid lines to create 12 flaps. Apply glue to the back of the center section to attach it to a notebook page.

If desired, this template can be modified to create smaller flap books by cutting off any number of rows from the bottom. You can also create a tall flap book by cutting off the flaps on the left side.

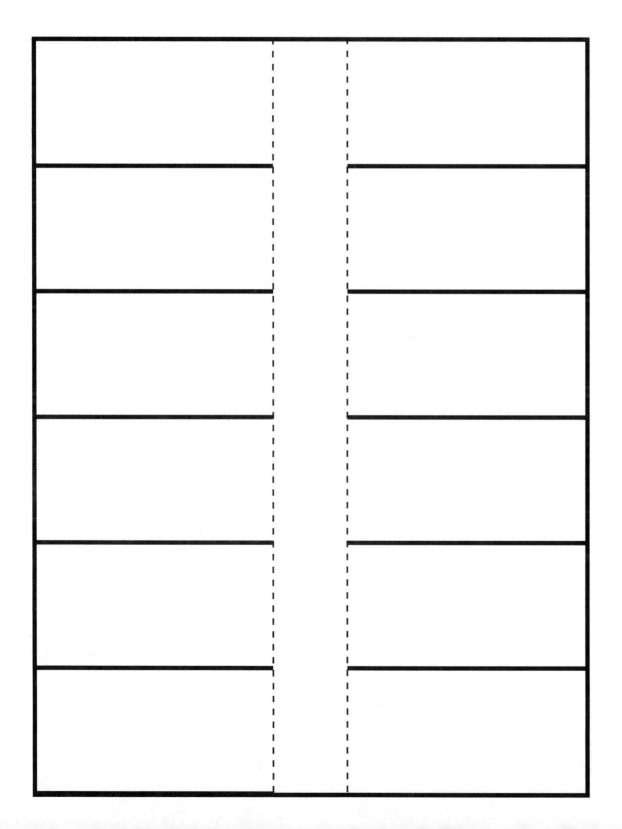

Shaped Flaps

Cut out each shaped flap. Apply glue to the back of the narrow section to attach it to a notebook page.

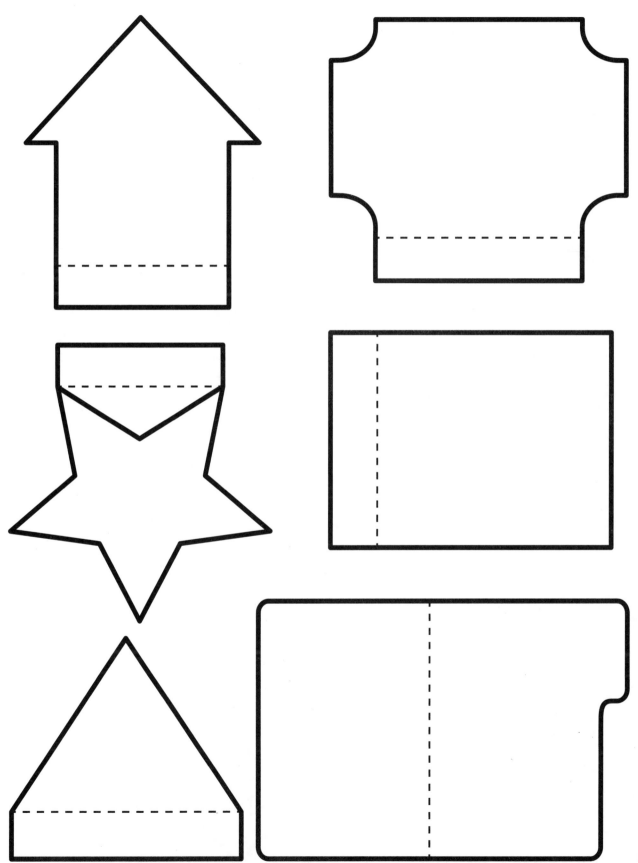

Shaped Flaps

Interlocking Booklet

Cut out the booklet on the solid lines, including the short vertical lines on the top and bottom flaps. Then, fold the top and bottom flaps toward the center, interlocking them using the small vertical cuts. Apply glue to the back of the center panel to attach it to a notebook page.

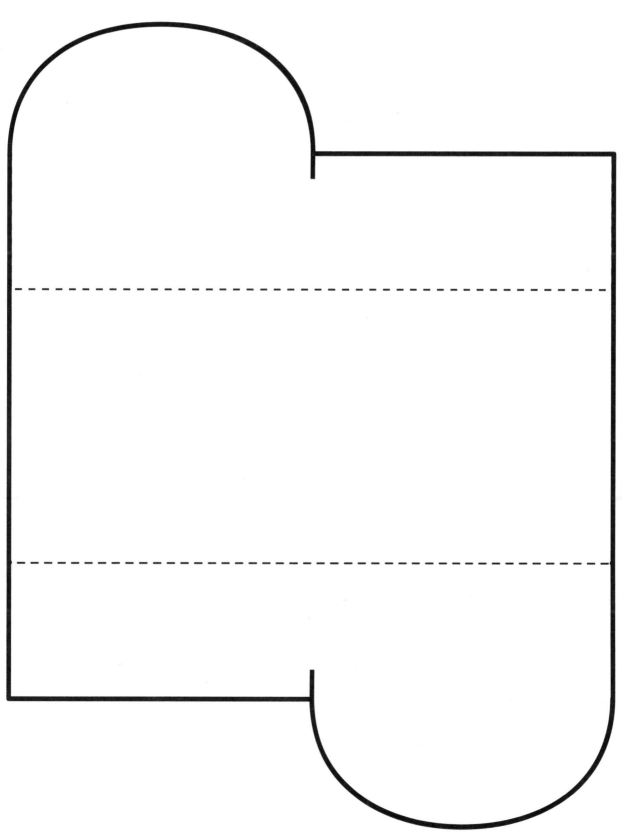

Four-Flap Petal Fold

Cut out the shape on the solid lines. Then, fold the flaps toward the center. Apply glue to the back of the center panel to attach it to a notebook page.

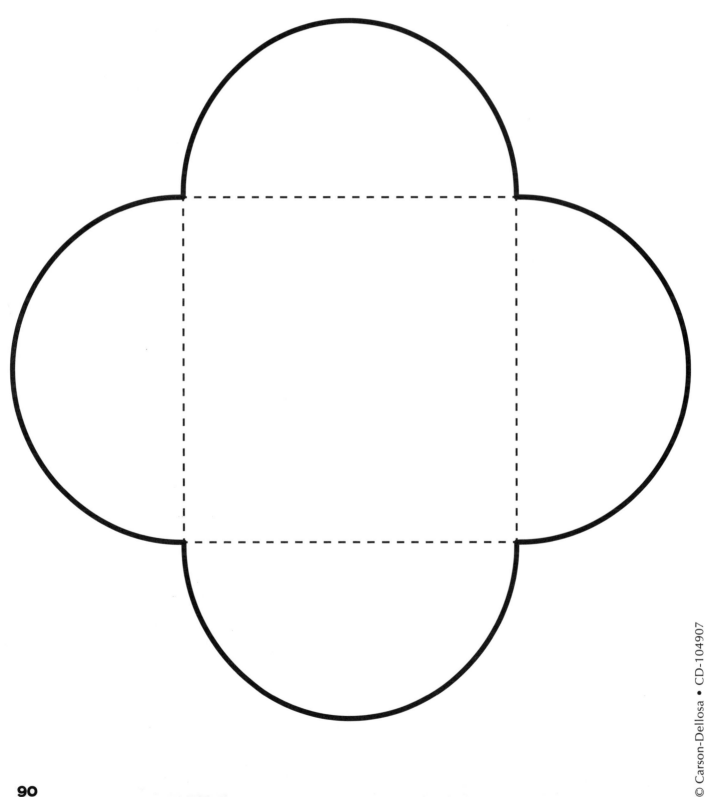

Six-Flap Petal Fold

Cut out the shape on the solid lines. Then, fold the flaps toward the center and back out. Apply glue to the back of the center panel to attach it to a notebook page.

Accordion Folds

Cut out the accordion pieces on the solid lines. Fold on the dashed lines, alternating the fold direction. Apply glue to the back of the last section to attach it to a notebook page.

You may modify the accordion books to have more or fewer pages by cutting off extra pages or by having students glue the first and last panels of two accordion books together.

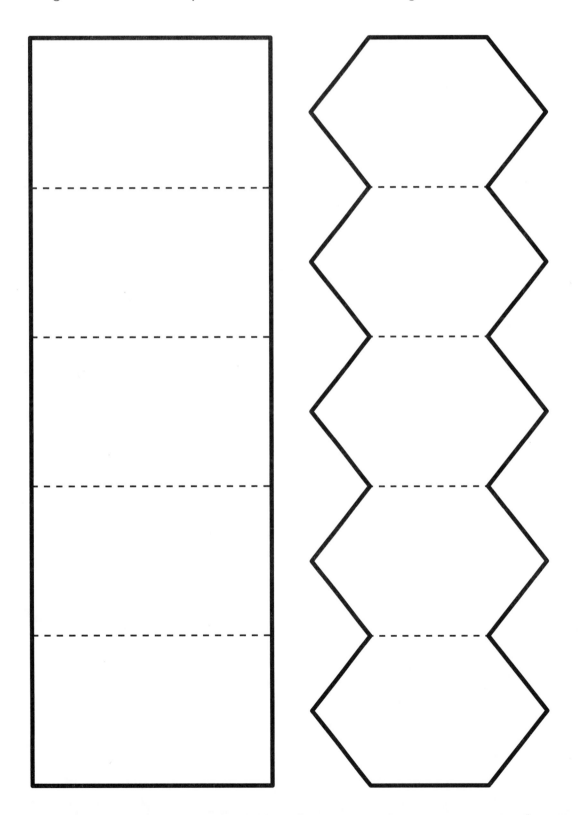

Accordion Folds

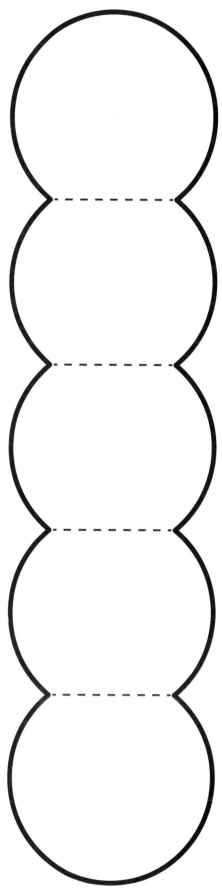

Clamshell Fold

Cut out the clamshell fold on the solid lines. Fold and unfold the piece on the three dashed lines. With the piece oriented so that the folds form an X with a horizontal line through it, pull the left and right sides together at the fold line. Then, keeping the sides touching, bring the top edge down to meet the bottom edge. You should be left with a triangular shape that unfolds into a square. Apply glue to the back of the triangle to attach the clamshell to a notebook page.

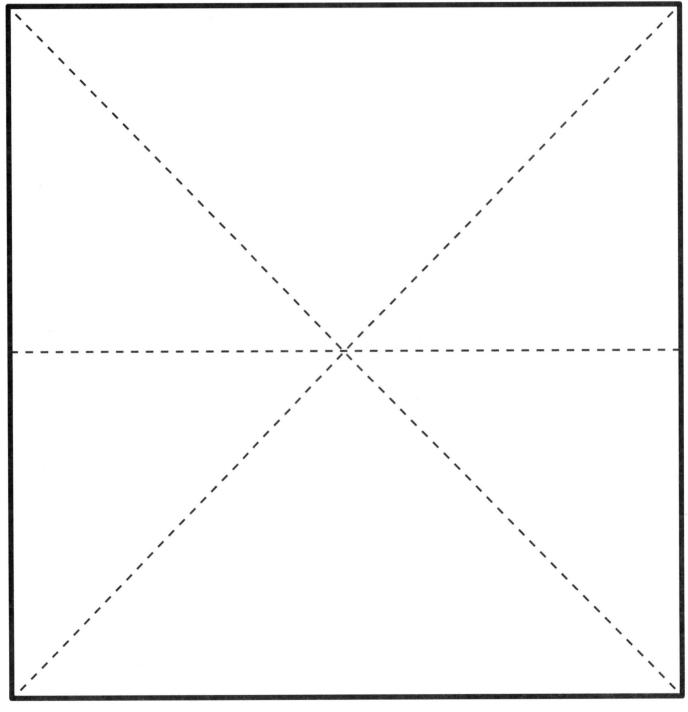

Puzzle Pieces

Cut out each puzzle along the solid lines to create a three- or four-piece puzzle. Apply glue to the back of each puzzle piece to attach it to a notebook page. Alternately, apply glue only to one edge of each piece to create flaps.

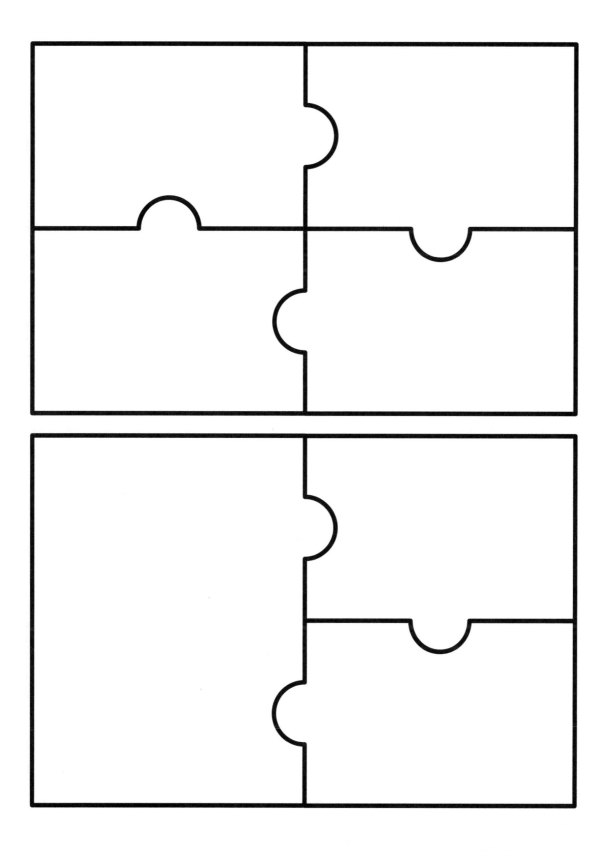

Flip Book

Cut out the two rectangular pieces on the solid lines. Fold each rectangle on the dashed lines. Fold the piece with the gray glue section so that it is inside the fold. Apply glue to the gray glue section and place the other folded rectangle on top so that the folds are nested and create a book with four cascading flaps. Make sure that the inside pages are facing up so that the edges of both pages are visible. Apply glue to the back of the book to attach it to a notebook page.

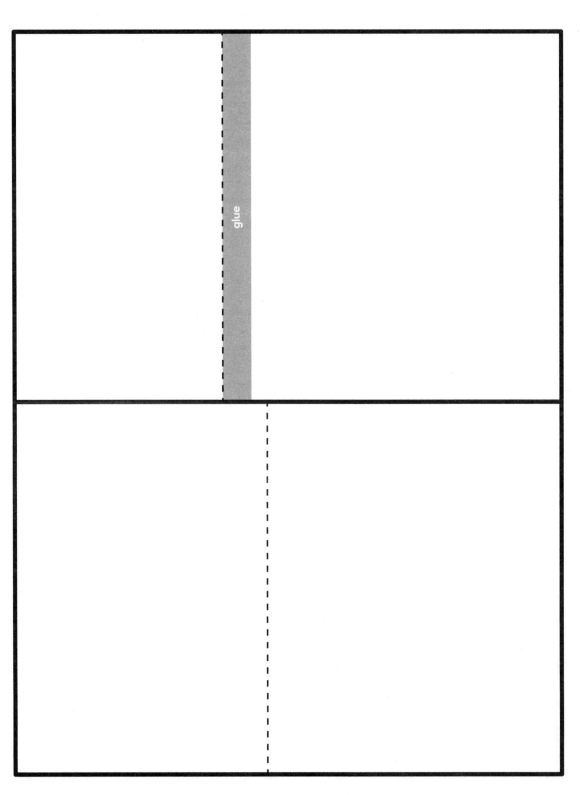

glue